Eminem

Titles in the People in the News series include:

Adam Sandler	Michael Crichton
Arnold Schwarzenegger	Michael Jackson
Ben Affleck	Nicolas Cage
Bill Gates	The Osbournes
Bono	Prince William
Britney Spears	Reese Witherspoon
Elijah Wood	Robin Williams
Garth Brooks	Sandra Bullock
George W. Bush	Steven Spielberg
Jennifer Love Hewitt	Sting
Jim Carrey	Tiger Woods
J.K. Rowling	Tim Allen
Johnny Depp	Tom Cruise
John Travolta	Tony Blair
Madonna	Will Smith

Eminem

by Stephanie Lane

LUCENT
BOOKS

THOMSON

———— ✦ ————™

GALE

San Diego • Detroit • New York • San Francisco • Cleveland
New Haven, Conn. • Waterville, Maine • London • Munich

For more information, contact
Lucent Books
27500 Drake Rd.
Farmington Hills, MI 48331-3535
Or you can visit our Internet site at http://www.gale.com

LIBRARY OF CONGRESS CATALOGING-IN-PUBLICATION DATA

Lane, Stephanie, 1975–
  Eminem / by Stephanie Lane.
    v. cm. — (People in the news)
  Includes bibliographical references (p. 101) and index.
  Contents: A controversial talent—Early hardships—Meet Slim Shady—Success and
controversy—Professional success, personal failures—Marshall Mathers takes no
prisoners—Going Hollywood—Looking forward.
    ISBN 1-59018-449-1 (hardback : alk. paper)
    1. Eminem (Musician)—Juvenile literature. 2. Rap musicians—United
States—Biography—Juvenile literature. [1. Eminem (Musician) 2.
Musicians. 3. Rap (Music)] I. Title. II. People in the news (series.)
  ML3930.E45L3 2004
    782.421649'092—dc22

                                                            2003020665

Table of Contents

Foreword

F̲AME AND CELEBRITY are alluring. People are drawn to those who walk in fame's spotlight, whether they are known for great accomplishments or for notorious deeds. The lives of the famous pique public interest and attract attention, perhaps because their experiences seem in some ways so different from, yet in other ways so similar to, our own.

Newspapers, magazines, and television regularly capitalize on this fascination with celebrity by running profiles of famous people. For example, television programs such as *Entertainment Tonight* devote all of their programming to stories about entertainment and entertainers. Magazines such as *People* fill their pages with stories of the private lives of famous people. Even newspapers, newsmagazines, and television news frequently delve into the lives of well-known personalities. Despite the number of articles and programs, few provide more than a superficial glimpse at their subjects.

Lucent's People in the News series offers young readers a deeper look into the lives of today's newsmakers, the influences that have shaped them, and the impact they have had in their fields of endeavor and on other people's lives. The subjects of the series hail from many disciplines and walks of life. They include authors, musicians, athletes, political leaders, entertainers, entrepreneurs, and others who have made a mark on modern life and who, in many cases, will continue to do so for years to come.

These biographies are more than factual chronicles. Each book emphasizes the contributions, accomplishments, or deeds that have brought fame or notoriety to the individual and shows how that person has influenced modern life. Authors portray their subjects in a realistic, unsentimental light. For example, Bill Gates—the cofounder and chief executive officer of the software giant Microsoft—has been instrumental in making personal computers the most vital tool of the modern age. Few dispute his business savvy, his perseverance, or his technical expertise, yet critics say he is ruthless in his dealings with competitors and driven more by his desire to maintain Microsoft's dominance in the computer industry than by an interest in furthering technology.

In these books, young readers will encounter inspiring stories about real people who achieved success despite enormous obstacles. Oprah Winfrey—the most powerful, most watched, and wealthiest woman on television today—spent the first six years of her life in the care of her grandparents while her unwed mother sought work and a better life elsewhere. Her adolescence was colored by promiscuity, pregnancy at age fourteen, rape, and sexual abuse.

Each author documents and supports his or her work with an array of primary and secondary source quotations taken from diaries, letters, speeches, and interviews. All quotes are footnoted to show readers exactly how and where biographers derive their information and provide guidance for further research. The quotations enliven the text by giving readers eyewitness views of the life and accomplishments of each person covered in the People in the News series.

In addition, each book in the series includes photographs, annotated bibliographies, timelines, and comprehensive indexes. For both the casual reader and the student researcher, the People in the News series offers insight into the lives of today's newsmakers—people who shape the way we live, work, and play in the modern age.

Introduction

A Controversial Talent

SINCE HE BURST onto the music scene in 1999 with the effervescent rap single "My Name Is," Eminem has been one of the most talked-about music artists of our time, inspiring both admiration for his technical rhyming and writing talents and shock at the offensive and sometimes brutal subjects that he chooses to rap about. No artist in the past decade has sparked quite as much controversy as Eminem, and no artist in recent history has been loved and hated by so many, in nearly equal measures.

Few critics, even those who have praised Eminem's talents, have been able to ignore the raw hate and anger present in Eminem's lyrics. At turns witty and shockingly violent, Eminem's songs have included ribald sexual fantasies about popular celebrities, angry and violent denunciations of homosexuals, and incredibly detailed fantasies about killing his ex-wife, Kim, and his mother, Debbie Mathers-Briggs. Music critics, feminist groups, and conservative politicians have all taken issue with Eminem's extremely frank and often offensive form of self-expression.

Perhaps Eminem's lyrics would attract less attention if his personal life didn't seem quite so contentious. While by all reports Eminem has settled down in recent years, his rise to the top included a bitter fight with his mother that ended their relationship; an angry and public separation and divorce from his wife, Kim; rumored drug use; and two incidents of assault with a concealed weapon that resulted in criminal charges. As his career exploded, Eminem was often in the news, and rarely was the news good. Eminem's personal trials left many wondering what kind of man would air such deep, bitter personal antagonism.

Eminem blames the volatility in his adult life on a difficult childhood. In interviews and in his music, Eminem speaks of growing up in Detroit's poorest and most dangerous neighborhoods, with a mother who never worked and rarely kept her family in one place for more than six months. Eminem has also hinted that his mother used drugs during his childhood and may have suffered

Eminem performs at the 2002 MTV Movie Awards. Since first attracting mainstream attention in 1999, Eminem has rocketed to success as a rapper, actor, and producer.

from Munchausen syndrome by proxy, a mental illness of parents who insist that their children are sick, often making them sick or forcing them to undergo painful tests and examinations, in order to gain attention for themselves. Eminem's mother denies all of these charges and suggests that Eminem is fabricating his hard-luck story to feed his hip-hop image. She even sued her son for $11 million for defamation of character, claiming that all of Eminem's complaints about her were lies. What was Eminem's childhood really like? Though it is known that Eminem and his mother lived in poor neighborhoods and rarely had much money, few details of his sensational claims have been verified.

Even as he's become one of the most talked-about musicians in recent memory, Eminem has kept the media guessing and cemented his image as an unpredictable and controversial public figure. Critics praise his lyric-writing talent, but condemn the violence in his music and his more childish public actions. Eminem is one of the rare celebrities who appears to be loved and hated in equal measures, both by the media and by the public at large. For every American who believes Eminem is a genius, there is at least one more who believes he is an untalented shock rapper, worthy of censure for his treatment of women and gays. While many people have strong opinions about Eminem, public opinion is certainly not uniform. The American public still appears unsure what to make of Eminem.

One thing that most critics and music fans agree on is that Eminem is exceptionally talented, both as a writer and as a rapper. Eminem's inventive lyrics and his dedication to his craft have garnered him critical raves on all of his albums, even as reviewers questioned the content of his songs. Eminem has proven himself as a rapper and a movie star, gained mainstream acceptance, and even appears to be settling down in his personal life. His fans, and the media, wait to see what he'll do next.

Chapter 1

Early Hardships

MARSHALL BRUCE MATHERS III, better known as rap performer Eminem, was born on October 17, 1972, in Kansas City, Missouri. He was the only child of the short-lived marriage of an absentee father and a teenage mother. From the very first days of his life, Marshall suffered many hardships that would later fuel the angry, over-the-top raps that made him a superstar in the music industry. As the child of a poor single mother, a child who, by his own accounts, was neglected by a substance-abusing parent, Eminem grew up with little sense of self-worth, and his anger and frustration would stay with him into adulthood.

Unprepared for Parenthood

Debbie Nelson, Marshall's mother, was only fifteen years old when she married the twenty-two-year-old Marshall Mathers Jr. in 1970. They met in Debbie's hometown of Kansas City, Missouri, performing in a band called Daddy Warbucks that played Ramada Inns along the Dakotas/Montana border. Debbie claims that she instantly fell in love, and they were married as soon as she reached the legal age (fifteen at the time in Missouri).

Marshall was born two years later, after seventy-three hours of painful labor for Debbie. She claims that the obstetrician charged only ninety dollars for prenatal care and delivery. She also claims that his medical care was so poor she nearly died in the process. When Marshall arrived safely, she was deeply grateful. But while Debbie may have been deeply in love, at seventeen she wasn't prepared for the challenges of marriage and motherhood.

Parenting was apparently too much for Eminem's father. When Eminem was only six months old, Marshall Jr. left his family

Eminem's mother Debbie Mathers-Briggs was only seventeen when her son was born. The rapper has claimed that she abused drugs and regularly beat him throughout his childhood.

to move to California, and contact between them ended. Debbie has since implied that Marshall Jr. was abusive toward his young family, and she suggested the separation. Whatever the reason for his departure, it seems that Marshall's father never looked back. As a teen, Marshall would write letters to his father, but they were all returned unopened.

Frequent Moves

Debbie Mathers and the young Marshall moved frequently and often lived in poor, crime-ridden neighborhoods. Marshall recalled his younger years to *SPIN* magazine:

> When I was five we moved to a real bad part of Detroit. I was getting beat up a lot, so we moved back to K.C., then back to Detroit again when I was 11. My mother couldn't afford to raise me, but then she had my little brother, so when we moved back to Michigan, we were just staying wherever we could, with my grandmother or whatever family would put us up. I know my mother tried to do the

The Mystery of Debbie Mathers-Briggs

In lyrics and in interviews, Eminem has suggested that his mother suffers from Munchausen syndrome by proxy, a mental illness in which a mother provokes illness or injury in her child to get attention and sympathy for herself. While Eminem has not referred to any specific incidents involving himself, Salon.com reports that Debbie Mathers-Briggs was accused in 1996 of abusing her younger son, Nathan, by the school officials in Eminem's old Detroit neighborhood of St. Clair Shores. According to M.L. Elrick's Salon.com article "Eminem's Dirty Secrets," a social worker claimed that Mathers-Briggs exhibited signs of Munchausen syndrome by proxy, and added that she "exhibits a very suspicious, almost paranoid personality." School officials claimed that Mathers-Briggs accused her neighbors of beating Nathan, blowing up her mailbox, and killing her dog in a satanic ritual. She also told them that video cameras were monitoring her from the trees surrounding her house and that an enemy had sent her a tarantula in the mail. After Nathan spent a year in foster homes, Mathers-Briggs pleaded no contest to reduced charges that she had displayed emotional instability and failed Nathan by keeping him out of school and isolating him from other children, and Nathan was returned to her custody.

"She was a pretty good mother," her defense attorney, Betsy Mellos, claims. "If anything, she was overprotective." Mathers-Briggs herself supports this claim, telling Elrick, "Anything Marshall wanted he got. I sheltered him too much and I think there's a little resentment from that." Her brother, Tom Nelson, agrees. But her ex-boyfriends tell a different story. "She is lying about the drugs and stuff," Fred Samra Jr., Nathan's estranged father, claims: "You would not believe the [stuff Eminem] has been through."

best she could, but I was bounced around so much–it seemed like we moved every two or three months. I'd go to, like, six different schools in one year.[1]

In Detroit, when Marshall was eleven, his mother gave birth to another son, Marshall's half brother Nathan, but there was still no male adult present in the household. Eminem has said that his mother never worked, and the family got by on public assistance and the support of friends and relatives. The constant moving around, and switching from school to school, made it difficult for Marshall to make friends. He describes his younger self as sensitive and introverted, often retreating into comic books or television. "I didn't really start opening up until eighth grade, going into ninth,"[2] Marshall recalls.

Violence and Bullying

As a white kid in the mostly black east side of Detroit, Marshall was often a target of bullying. "I was always getting jumped on, dog!" he recalls. "I lived in a [bad] neighborhood where there was always some kind of drama."[3]

When Marshall was in the fourth grade, he was often tormented by a sixth-grade bully named D'Angelo Bailey. That name will be familiar to Marshall's fans because, as Eminem, he would later turn a violent beating at Bailey's hand into the subject of the song "Brain Damage." As Marshall later commented, "Everything in the song is true. . . . D'Angelo Bailey–no one called him D'Angelo–came running from across the yard and hit me so hard into this snowbank that I blacked out."[4] He eventually came to and managed to get home on his own, but later that day he began bleeding from the ear and his mother rushed him to the hospital. "He had a cerebral hemorrhage and was in and out of consciousness for five days," his mother recalls. "The doctors had given up on him, but I wouldn't give up on my son."[5]

Another incident took place in a parking lot when Marshall was a little older. He recalls, "I was walking home from my boy's house, through the Bel-Air Shopping Center. All these black dudes rode by in a car, flippin' me off. I flipped them off back, they drove away, and I didn't think nothin' of it." But the toughs apparently parked

The Wrath of D'Angelo Bailey

Eminem claims that in grade school a boy named D'Angelo Bailey made his life miserable through constant bullying and beatings. Bailey's most severe beating, which landed Eminem in the hospital with a cerebral hemorrhage, was immortalized (if somewhat exaggerated) on the track "Brain Damage" from *The Slim Shady LP*. While Bailey admitted in Anthony Bozza's *Rolling Stone* article "Eminem Blows Up" that he did occasionally beat up Marshall Mathers, he was sufficiently offended by his portrayal in "Brain Damage" that in December 2001 he filed a $1 million defamation lawsuit against Eminem.

In October 2003, Judge Deborah Servitto issued a ruling dismissing Bailey's case. She asserted that Eminem's raps are clearly exaggerated and not meant to be taken seriously. According to the October 20, 2003, Associated Press article "Eminem Wins Defamation Lawsuit," in a humorous nod to rap, Servitto also issued a ten-stanza rhyme explaining her ruling. It read in part, "It is therefore this court's ultimate position, that Eminem is entitled to summary disposition."

the car. "One dude came up, hit me in the face and knocked me down. Then he pulled out a gun. I ran right out my shoes, dog. I thought that's what they wanted."[6]

Marshall was saved when another motorist pulled over and produced another gun that scared the boys away. The man took pity on Marshall and drove him home.

Discovering Rap

When Marshall was nine, his Uncle Ronnie (Ronnie Polkingham, Debbie's younger brother) gave him a gift that would change his life. Uncle Ronnie was only a few months older than Marshall, and the boys were very close. The gift was the sound track to a breakdancing-exploitation movie called *Breakin' It*. It contained the track "Reckless" by Ice T, the first rap song Marshall ever heard. Marshall listened to the album over and over. "I was fascinated,"[7] he recalls.

Over time, Marshall's rap record collection expanded. He began listening to rappers like Run-DMC, LL Cool J, the Fat Boys, and the Beastie Boys. When he first heard the Beastie Boys, Marshall recalls, "I didn't even know they were white. I just thought they were dope, the craziest stuff I'd ever heard. Then I

Eminem onstage with members of his Detroit-based rap group D-12. Eminem has frequently encountered prejudice as a white rapper in a predominately black genre.

saw a video and realized they were white. It made me think, 'Hey, I can do this.'"[8]

Marshall's love of rap music and desire to become a rapper only deepened over the years. "From LL Cool J to the Fat Boys . . . I was fascinated. When LL first came out with 'I'm Bad,' I wanted to do it, to rhyme. Standing in front of the mirror, I wanted to be like LL."[9]

Marshall began composing his own rhymes when he was four-teen. At this point, he also adopted the moniker Eminem, taken from his own initials (M.M.: Marshall Mathers). Soon he was ready to take his act out in public.

Early Rapping

Eminem's rapping career began in the cafeteria of neighboring Osborne High School, where he and his friend DJ Proof would sneak in to take part in lunchtime rhyming contests. From the very beginning, Eminem's rapping skills were obvious. "It was like *White Men Can't Jump*," Proof remembers. "Everybody thought he'd be easy to beat, and they got smoked every time."[10]

The fact that Eminem was a white rapper in a mostly black genre hindered him at first. "I'd hang out on the corner where kids would be rhyming, and when I tried to get in there, I'd get dissed," he recalled to *SPIN* magazine. "A little color issue de-veloped, and as I got old enough to hit the clubs, it got really bad. I wasn't that dope yet, but I knew I could rhyme, so I'd get on the open mics . . . and a couple of times I was booed off the stage."[11]

Eminem and Proof's open mic contest of choice was the Saturday night contest at the Hip-Hop Shop on Detroit's West 7 Mile Road, the center of the local rap community. Sometimes, Eminem recalls, "I'd get booed as soon as I started speaking. But once they heard me rhyme, they'd soon shut up."[12]

Still, the racial issue bothered Eminem:

> When you're a little kid, you don't see color, and the fact that my friends were black never crossed my mind. It never became an issue until I was a teenager and started trying to rap. Then I'd notice that a lot of [the black rappers] al-ways had my back, but somebody always had to say to them, "Why do you have to stick up for the white boy?"[13]

Eminem was in an odd situation. "There was a while when I was feeling like, 'Damn, if I'd just been born black, I would not have to go through all this,'" he recalls. "But I'm not ignorant—I know how it must be when a black person goes to get a regular job in society."[14]

Fortunately for Eminem, his talent and the support of his friends led him through the tensest contests. At this point, Eminem was completely obsessed with rapping. He got a job as a cook at the local restaurant Gilbert's Lounge, where he made $5.50 an hour. But as he worked the restaurant job, his mind often wandered to rhymes. "I like to throw my ideas just scattered onto paper. When I was busing tables I'd write 'em on my hand or on receipts."[15]

Rapping in various freestyle contests enabled Eminem to meet other young rappers with talent. Soon he began performing with the groups the New Jacks and Soul Intent. With his buddy Proof, Eminem created the group the Dirty Dozen or D-12. D-12 is very dear to Eminem's heart, and he still performs with them today.

A Tough Decision and a Devastating Tragedy

Eminem attended Lincoln High School in nearby Warren, Michigan. With his interest in school completely overshadowed by his love of rap, Eminem decided to drop out of high school at seventeen. He had failed the ninth grade three years in a row. "That wasn't because I was stupid or nothing," he says now. "It was just because I never went to school. I was enrolled, but I just never went. I always wanted to rap."[16] At seventeen, after he dropped out of school, Eminem moved in with Kim Scott, his girlfriend.

In 1993, when Eminem was twenty, his mother called him at a friend's house one day to deliver devastating news: Uncle Ronnie had killed himself while suffering from depression. Eminem was devastated. "Uncle Ronnie was like my big brother," he says. "He knew loads about music. He became my mentor. When he died I didn't talk for days. I couldn't even go to the funeral."[17] He quit rapping for one year following Uncle Ronnie's death.

A New Inspiration

Over the next six years, Eminem worked at such menial jobs as sweeping floors and cleaning toilets while he struggled to improve his rap skills and get his big break.

On Christmas Day 1995, Eminem received a new and extremely potent source of inspiration–the birth of his daughter with Kim, Hailie Jade. "You know I think my little girl was the real wakeup call for me," he says. "She made me . . . make something

of my life and try ten quadrillion times harder than I had before."[18]
Eminem and Kim chose not to marry at this point, but their de-
votion to their new daughter was unquestionable.

From that point on, Eminem was driven by desire to give
Hailie the childhood that he never had:

> I was so scared I wouldn't be able to raise Hailie and sup-
> port her as a father should. I had nothing at the time. But

*Eminem's ex-wife Kimberly Mathers has been the inspiration for many
of Eminem's darkest lyrics.*

I think parenthood comes naturally to me. I mean, in a lot of ways I raised my little brother who was born when I was eleven. And I wanted to be a father to Hailie and not do what my dad did to me.[19]

The new father had also taken a new step professionally, recording his first album.

Infinite

Marky and Jeff Bass, the Detroit hip-hop producers known as the Funky Bass Team or FBT Productions, had heard Eminem freestyling on a late-night radio show on local station WHYT. Immediately impressed, they invited him to record his first album in their studio.

Due to the low budget productions of his first few albums, Eminem made do with recording in local studios such as this one on West 8 Mile Road in Ferndale, Michigan.

The result was *Infinite*, which was released on local Detroit label Web Entertainment in 1996. It was unsuccessful, both critically and commercially. *Infinite* "was way hip-hopped out, like Nas and AZ–that rhyme style was real in at the time," Eminem says. In retrospect, he sees the album's flaws. "I've always been a smart-ass comedian, and that's why it wasn't a good album."[20]

Eminem offered other reasons why *Infinite* wasn't an artistic success:

> It was a growing stage. I was trying to figure out my style and how to sound on the mic. Really, it was a demo that just got pressed up. I made it right before my daughter was born, so that was all I talked about. It wasn't a good album. After that record, every rhyme I wrote got angrier and angrier. It was because of the feedback I got. It just made me so annoyed.[21]

When *Infinite* failed to launch a rapping career for Eminem, he was forced to confront the conditions his family was living in.

Rock Bottom

Kim, Hailie, and Eminem lived in one of the most run down, crime-prone neighborhoods in Detroit. Their apartment was burglarized five times, Kim recalls: "I went through four TVs and five VCRs in two years." One of the family's burglars was bold enough to come back to their apartment just to make himself a sandwich. "He left the peanut butter, jelly . . . out and didn't steal nothing. . . . But then he came back again and took everything but the couches and beds. The pillows, clothes, silverware–everything."[22]

At one point, Kim, Hailie, and Eminem were evicted from their apartment because they could not afford to pay rent. Kim left with Hailie to stay with her mother, which shamed Eminem: "[Kim's] looking at me like, 'You're supposed to be the man, you're supposed to be taking care of your family and you can't even feed yourself.'"[23]

Around Christmas 1996, Eminem's relationship with Kim was suffering, *Infinite* was failing to launch his career, and he was fired from his job at the Gilbert Lounge. Eminem fell into a deep depression. He made a potentially suicidal gesture the night the track "Rock Bottom" was written:

> I was supposed to be getting a deal from a record label and I found out that the guy who had been saying he was going to get us the deal worked in the mailroom and he was nobody. . . . I took a bunch of pills and puked them all up. . . . I don't know if I was necessarily trying to kill myself but I was just really depressed and kept thinking "more pills, more pills." I bet I took twenty pills in the course of two hours.[24]

Even if Eminem's overdose was not a deliberate suicide attempt, he thought he might die:

> I thought I was going to die for real. . . . My head was spinning, I remember the room looked like everything going in circles. . . . My boys looked out for me; they tried to keep my head up the next day because I was still depressed. We was all depressed because FBT had a lot of money invested in me and they didn't know if they were going to make their money back, so they were depressed. But they was trying to keep my head up because they knew what I was going through.[25]

But even as Eminem almost gave up hope, *Infinite* was making some progress.

First Commercial Success

"Searchin'," one of the tracks on *Infinite*, received some airplay on the local urban station, WCHB. And while most reviews were virtual shrugs, there was the occasional gem, like these comments from Marc Kempf in an *Underground Soundz* review: "One of Em's tightest skills [is] his ability to hit back to back. [Rather than] rhyme the last syllable, Eminem will instead rhyme the last six syllables. . . . His mastery of the English language allows him to write coherent stories, not just freestyle ramblings that happen to rhyme."[26]

Eminem did a few live shows and radio performances to promote *Infinite*. He also competed in freestyle competitions around the country, which started a buzz beyond the Detroit scene. It was enough to land him a featured spot in *Source*'s influential "Unsigned Hype" column.

Infinite was also sent to Rap Coalition's Wendy Day, who invited Eminem to perform at the 1997 Rap Olympics in Los Angeles, a huge freestyle competition that got national exposure and attracted scouts from many different record labels. Eminem didn't know it yet, but the Rap Olympics—and a certain character named Slim Shady—were about to change his life.

Chapter 2

Meet Slim Shady

WHEN *INFINITE* FAILED to bring Eminem the fame and success that he dreamed of, he experienced frustration, shame, anger, and disappointment. Little did he know, those very dark emotions would give him the inspiration to turn his career around. When Eminem developed a new, angrier, brutally honest persona by the name of Slim Shady, and began writing songs about personal slights and rapping frankly about his most private frustrations, he was rocketed on the road to success.

The Creation of Slim Shady

In the months before the 1997 Rap Olympics, things were not going well for Eminem, professionally or personally. His first album had failed to connect with audiences. His relationship with Kim was strained by their dire financial situation, and he felt guilty for not being able to support his family. One day in early 1997, Eminem's frustration and anger led him to inspiration. If he used these dark emotions in his raps, he could create a whole new persona for himself. Eminem might never publicly discuss his frustrations in his marriage or his darkest, most violent fantasies. But this other persona would. He would look, dress, and act like Eminem—except for one important difference. This persona would say all the terrible things Eminem would censor himself from saying. And this persona would be called Slim Shady.

With his usual candor, Eminem recalls, "I was [on the toilet]. I swear to God. And the . . . name just popped into my head. Then I started thinkin' of twenty million things that rhymed with it."[27] Eminem knew that he'd had a major breakthrough. He immediately got up and called all of his friends.

Slim Shady became the second of Marshall's alter egos. The real Marshall Mathers was the poor, often-bullied kid who'd grown up on the streets of Detroit. Then Marshall emerged as Eminem, the white rapper who commanded respect at freestyle contests all over the city. And now, there was Slim Shady—the angry, crass, violent, and often offensive persona who seemed to give voice to all of Marshall's and Eminem's most reprehensible thoughts.

Of his least socially acceptable persona, Eminem says: "Slim Shady is just the evil thoughts that come into my head. Things I shouldn't be thinking about. It's just me—a different side of me, but not a separate character. Slim Shady is the dark, evil, creatively sick part of me."[28]

The creation of Slim Shady gave Eminem a no-holds-barred way to air personal grievances. "When I started using the whole Slim Shady name," he recalls, "it gave me a chance to take what was wrong with my life and turn it back on [to others]."[29]

Dressed in one of his Slim Shady outfits, Eminem performs in 2000. Slim Shady is Eminem's alter ego and the outlet for his most offensive thoughts.

The Slim Shady EP

Months before he left for the 1997 Rap Olympics, Eminem took his new Slim Shady persona into the studio. Eminem recorded a ten-track extended-play CD, *The Slim Shady EP*, on Web Entertainment. He and some fans from the Web label pressed up enough promo copies to send out to all the prominent rap-industry figures in Detroit. The disc got some great feedback from Detroit record store owners.

Eminem's original idea for the CD cover was a close-up of his own naked rear, intended as an insult to all the critics of *Infinite*. Eventually, Eminem and Web Entertainment settled on different cover art: a photo of Eminem smashing a mirror. Eminem explains:

> I had this whole Slim Shady concept of being two different people, having two different sides of me. One of them I was trying to let go and I looked at the mirror and smashed it. That was the whole intro of *The Slim Shady EP*. Slim Shady was coming to haunt me, was coming to haunt Eminem.[30]

Most of the contents of *The Slim Shady EP* would be familiar to fans of Eminem's first widely released album, *The Slim Shady LP*. There were early versions of the songs "Just Don't Give a F——" and "If I Had," as well as a song called "Just the Two of Us," an early version of what would become Eminem's infamously violent song about Kim, "97 Bonnie & Clyde." On the track "Mommy," Eminem berated his mother for her shortcomings in raising him. In addition, D-12 members Bizarre and Swift made guest appearances on the track "No One's Iller."

After the disappointment of *Infinite*, Eminem was determined to get it right this time. "I had nothing to lose but something to gain," he recalls. "On *The Slim Shady EP*, I just lashed out at everyone who'd talked bad about me."[31]

The Rap Olympics

In the summer of 1997, Eminem was invited to the Rap Olympics in Los Angeles. The Rap Olympics were a long-standing freestyle competition. The first prize was five hundred dollars and a Rolex watch. Eminem desperately needed the cash, but he needed the exposure even more. He'd spent years chasing his dream of becoming a rap star, and he knew that if he didn't make it big soon, he was going to have to find some other way to support his family. "I felt, 'It's my time to shine,'" Eminem recalls of the competition. "'I have to rip this.' At that time, I felt that it was a life or death situation."[32]

There were fifty contestants in that year's competition, but Eminem was an electrifying performer. He made it to the final round with ease. But when it came down to Eminem and one other rapper, the judges decided against Eminem. He was given second prize, and he was devastated. "Em really looked like he was going to cry,"[33] recalls Paul Rosenberg, his manager.

Being in Los Angeles allowed Eminem to make an important radio appearance. While he was in town for the Rap Olympics, Eminem freestyled on Sway and Tech's *Wake Up Show* on Los Angeles's 92.3 (The Beat). His performance caught the attention of some important music-industry players and earned him the title of *Wake Up Show*'s 1997 Freestyle Performer of the Year. But perhaps the most important thing to happen at the Rap Olympics, although Eminem had no idea of its importance at the time, was that a copy of *The Slim Shady EP* was placed in the hands of Interscope Records executive Jimmy Iovine.

Interscope had recently given rap-industry giant Dr. Dre his own label at Interscope records, called Aftermath. Dr. Dre knew the importance of launching a new music label, and he was searching for something "different" for the launch of Aftermath. A few weeks after the Rap Olympics, Dr. Dre was visiting Iovine's home when he noticed *The Slim Shady EP* lying on the floor of his garage. Dr. Dre was instantly attracted to the cover, and he picked the disc up and insisted on listening to it with Iovine. He couldn't believe what he was hearing. "Not too many people can turn me on off the first listen, without a visual," Dr. Dre recalls. "His [stuff] was complete. I could tell that he spent time on his lyrics and that he was a perfectionist with how he delivered them." Dr. Dre knew that he had to find this talented rapper. "In my entire career in the music industry," he says, "I have never found anything from a demo tape or a CD. But when Jimmy played me this tape, I said 'Find him. Now.'"[34]

Offending Sister Tamu

In early October 1999, while he was working on *The Marshall Mathers LP,* Eminem made a controversial appearance on the popular college radio station KALX 90.7 FM in Berkeley, California. The host of the Sunday morning show on which he was a guest, Sister Tamu, sat Eminem down before they went on the air and advised him to keep his comments and his freestyles clean, so as not to offend her audience. While the interview went well—though Eminem was rankled by a few of Sister Tamu's references to his race—trouble began when Sister Tamu began accepting calls from listeners. One listener begged Eminem to show off his freestyling skills, and Eminem obliged, including a line in his rap about slapping a pregnant woman. Sister Tamu promptly pulled him off the air, threw him out of the studio, and later, while promising to never, ever invite him back on her show, broke her copy of *The Slim Shady LP* in half on the air.

Needless to say, Eminem was blown away when he heard that Dr. Dre was interested in working with him.

It was an honor to hear the words out of Dre's mouth that he liked my [record]. Growing up, I was one of the biggest fans of N.W.A., from putting on the sunglasses and looking in the mirror and lip-synching to wanting to be Dr. Dre, to be Ice Cube. This is the biggest hip-hop producer ever.[35]

Eminem signed a recording contract with Aftermath Records in January 1998. One of Eminem's closest friends, D-12 member Bizarre, recalls: "He was missing for three weeks. Nowhere to be found. Then he just up and called me out of the blue: 'Yo, man, I just signed with Dr. Dre. He's got this fresh condo out here; you got to see it!'"[36]

Eminem's career was finally taking off, but working with one of the biggest rap producers of all time was a little intimidating. He recalls: "It was a dream come true, but I had to shake the butterflies at first. I had an anxiousness to just get in there and show him what I could do. I knew Dre was basically putting his credibility on the line for me, because if I came out wack, it could destroy his career."[37]

Ultimately, Eminem's discovery came just in time. If he hadn't found success soon after the Rap Olympics, Eminem would have had to find some other way to support his family: "I would definitely have quit in '97 if it hadn't been for Dre. My daughter was one year old at the time and I couldn't afford to buy her diapers. I didn't have a job. I didn't have a high school diploma. I was basically going nowhere. So when I say Dre saved my life, I mean he literally saved my life. I owe him everything."[38]

Legendary hip-hop star and producer Dr. Dre is credited with recognizing and developing Eminem's musical talent.

Dre and Eminem

From the minute they set foot in the studio together, Dr. Dre and
Eminem realized that they were the perfect partners. Eminem
recalls:

> Ever since the first day we got into the studio and got
> down, I knew we had a chemistry. Every beat Dre would
> make I had a rhyme for. And Dre made me better. He
> showed me how to deliver rhymes over a beat, and he
> showed me that you stick with something until you have
> it just how you want it.[39]

Eminem's first single, the song that would become his breakout
hit, "My Name Is," was recorded within one hour of Dre and
Eminem walking through the studio door.

Eminem admits that drugs played a part in these first few
recording sessions with Dr. Dre. According to Anthony Bozza, a
reporter for *Rolling Stone* who did a lengthy interview with Eminem
shortly after *The Slim Shady LP* was released, Eminem and Dre
were frequent users of Ecstasy. "I wrote two songs for the next
album on Ecstasy," Eminem told Bozza. "[Stuff] about bouncing
off walls, going straight through 'em, falling down twenty stories. Crazy. That's what we do when I'm in the studio with Dre."

Dr. Dre agrees. "It's true. . . . We get in there, get bugged
out, stay in the studio for . . . two days. Then you're dead for
three days. Then you wake up, pop the tape in, like, 'Let me
see what I've done.'"[40]

Dr. Dre and Eminem worked so well together, drugs or no, that
Dre later invited Eminem to contribute to his own *2001* album.

Marketing *Slim Shady*

Once Eminem's wide-release debut album, *The Slim Shady LP*,
was recorded, Aftermath Records began to think very carefully
about how to market its new talent to the music-buying public.
The most obvious thing about Eminem, and the trait that set him
apart from most other rappers on the market, was that Eminem
was white. As Dr. Dre and Aftermath executives considered
Eminem's debut, they weren't sure whether his race would be a

help or a hindrance. "It's some very awkward [stuff]," Dre said at the time. "It's like seeing a black guy doing country & western, know what I'm saying?"[41] At the time, in the era following the rise and fall of the pop-influenced, media-styled Vanilla Ice, it was extremely difficult to gain respect as a white rapper. "People have tried to play every white rapper that comes out like a gimmick,"[42] Eminem said at the time. Eminem himself was annoyed by the skepticism he encountered as a white rapper.

> Nobody has the right to tell me what kind of music to listen to or how to dress or how to act or how to talk; if people want to make jokes, well [forget] 'em. I lived this [life], you know what I'm sayin'? And if you hear an Eminem record, you're gonna know the minute that it comes on that this ain't no fluke.[43]

Ultimately, Dr. Dre believed that Eminem's race could work for them.

> If you're dope, you're dope. I didn't know Eminem was white until I met him, but I saw it as an edge, that we could get away with lyrical stuff that we wouldn't normally be able to get away with. And I don't care if you're purple. If you can kick it, I'll work with you.[44]

Dr. Dre believed in Eminem's talent so fervently, he made a decision to do something unusual in the music world when launching a new artist: He didn't want Eminem to collaborate with any better-known artists on *The Slim Shady LP*. He believed that Eminem's talent spoke for itself.

A few months before the release of *The Slim Shady LP*, Aftermath stirred up interest in the album by sending Eminem on a national tour. They also released the pre-album single "Just Don't Give a F—," with "Brain Damage" as a B-side. The song would become a top-ten rap single in early 1999.

Aftermath also got an unprecedented amount of press for the album before it was released, with stories in *Rap Pages,* the *Source, SPIN, Stress, URB*, and *Vibe. SPIN* had some nice words to say: "Imaginatively unhinged and bearing a thesaurus full of

Eminem on Tupac

On September 13, 1996, the rap community was shocked by the news that top rapper Tupac Shakur had been killed in a sensational drive-by shooting in Las Vegas. Eminem had been listening to Tupac since he was seventeen years old, and particularly loved the songs "Dear Mama" and "Brenda's Got a Baby." He praises the artist and acknowledges Tupac's influence in Shaheem Reid's MTV.com article "Eminem: Reconstructing Tupac":

> I remember exactly where I was when I heard that Tupac died. . . . I was cooking in a restaurant. It was me, Kuniva and Kon Artis from D12. We all had the same job. There was a big TV screen. We all just kinda watched it, just dazed. . . . I just remember this feeling of gloominess. A lot of the people at the job that I worked at didn't understand Tupac or didn't understand the music. So they were look-ing at us like, "What? What's wrong? What's the big deal? Get over it." And it's like, "Nah, you don't, you don't understand. This is a re-ally [messed up] day." . . . There's a lot of things about Pac that stood out. Personality. I guess no matter what color you was or where you came from, you felt like you could relate to him. He made you feel like you knew him. I think that honestly, Tupac was the greatest songwriter that ever lived. He made it seem so *easy*. The emotion was there, and feeling, and everything he was trying to describe. You saw a picture that he was trying to paint. That's what I picked up from him, making your words so vivid that somebody can pic-ture them in their head.

Eminem was honored to be asked to produce several tracks for the 2003 documentary film *Tupac: Resurrection*.

Tupac Shakur is one of Eminem's biggest rap influences.

insults, Eminem comes off like a white-trash Don Rickles who grew up worshipping LL Cool J."[45] The *Los Angeles Times* did a major feature on Eminem on February 7, 1999, two weeks before the album's release.

Aftermath executives were thrilled by the advance buzz the album had created. They were so sure that the album was going to be a hit, they decided on an initial shipment of an unprecedented 1 million copies. All of the pieces were in place. Now all Dr. Dre and Eminem could do was wait and see if all their hard work would pay off.

Chapter 3

Success and Controversy

Wiтн тне wноlеhеаrтеd support of Dr. Dre and Aftermath Records, *The Slim Shady LP* was unleashed on an unsuspecting public. While the album sold record numbers, many critics were unsure how to react to lyrics of such rage and political incorrectness. America's introduction to Slim Shady was a love/hate affair, with Eminem experiencing phenomenal success in album sales and unrelenting controversy over his lyrics at the same time.

The Slim Shady LP's Release

The Slim Shady LP was released on February 22, 1999. With the single "My Name Is" already burning up the airwaves and in seemingly constant rotation on MTV, the album seemed destined for success, and *Slim Shady* didn't disappoint. It entered the Billboard charts as the number-two best-selling album in America, selling over five hundred thousand copies in just two weeks. Three months later, the sales were up to 2 million, and *The Slim Shady LP* had gone double platinum.

The sudden success was a little mind-boggling for Eminem.

> The transition of being a regular [guy] to now happens so fast. From the day we shot [the "My Name Is"] video, I remember [things] moving so fast. It was like I got the Buzz Clip on MTV, then ridiculous [stuff] started happening. Like, I went from being home all the time to never seeing my girl to being out on the road to [girls] throwing themselves at me. It was like a movie, the [stuff] you see in movies.[46]

There was no denying that America's love affair with Slim Shady had begun. In April 1999, Eminem graced the cover of *Rolling Stone*, the music industry bible, for the first time.

Songs

As Americans were buying up thousands of copies of *The Slim Shady LP*, they found themselves coming face to face with the Slim Shady character—a confrontational, angry, politically incorrect character who didn't hesitate to target women, gays, and celebrities with equally virulent phrases. The songs on *The Slim Shady LP* would encounter huge amounts of controversy, largely for Eminem's no-holds-barred lyrics.

The first single to be released from *The Slim Shady LP* was "My Name Is." Aftermath did everything they could to market the single to the general pop audience, creating an edited, profanity-free version of the song for radio play, and shooting a fun video that MTV ran nearly nonstop. But the original lyrics to "My Name Is"—those found on the album—caused controversy among listeners, parents, and music critics. In one song, Eminem discussed his desire to impregnate a Spice Girl, claimed to have "ripped

The Slim Shady LP

2,000,000

☐ Released on February 22, 1999

☐ Entered Billboard charts as the number two best-selling album in America

☐ Sold over five hundred thousand copies in first two weeks

500,000

☐ Sold over 2 million copies within the first three and a half months

Spending Eminem's Money

It's safe to say that Eminem is richer than he ever dreamed he could be. But Eminem claims that he's one multimillionaire who isn't interested in flaunting his wealth. He explains in Chuck Weiner's book, *Eminem: Talking:*

> I've got a Mustang and an Explorer. I don't want a Benz. I don't wear jewelry—that's not me. This [stuff] doesn't last forever and I don't want to wear my house around my neck or my car on my wrist. I'd rather invest and do the right things, make sure my daughter is put through college and she has an opportunity that I never had. I invest it in stocks and bonds. I've got my own record label, so I'm going to make that jump off the way that I want to.

Pamela Lee's [breasts] off," claimed to have stapled his English teacher's testicles to a stack of paper, insisted that "my mom does more dope than I do," and discussed his dreams of slitting his father's throat.[47]

In that one song, the world was introduced to Slim Shady.

"Rock Bottom" is the song that Eminem wrote on the night of his unsuccessful suicide attempt. It's a song that deals with deep depression and the feeling of not having the basic possessions that others seem to have.

"Brain Damage" harkens back to Eminem's unhappy days on the playground–specifically, the days in which he was harassed and beaten by a classmate named D'Angelo Bailey. "Brain Damage" recounts the incident, but changes a few key details. In the song, Eminem gets D'Angelo Bailey back with an equally savage beating. Also, in the song, Eminem's mother is blatantly unsympathetic to her son's plight. Finally, Eminem also embellishes his injury creatively–in "Brain Damage," young Eminem's brain falls out of his head and has to be sewn back in.

"If I Had" is a song that deals with Eminem's frustrations and feelings of inadequacy at being poor for so long before his rap career took off. Like "Rock Bottom," it's a sobering look at Eminem's state of mind before his discovery by Dr. Dre. "'If I Had' and 'Rock Bottom' are the real serious songs on that album," Eminem has said. "Those are the songs to show people what I really went through growing up."[48]

Perhaps the most controversial song on *The Slim Shady LP* is one called "97 Bonnie & Clyde." In the song, Eminem takes his daughter Hailie to the beach. When they get there, it gradually becomes clear that Eminem has killed his wife and Hailie's mother, Kim, and stuffed her body in the trunk. He and Hailie throw her body off the pier after he explains to Hailie that Kim wants to "go swimming."

The subject matter of "97 Bonnie & Clyde" might be chilling enough, but to make the song even more shocking, Eminem used Hailie's real voice (Hailie was three years old at the time) in the recording of the track. He sneaked her into the studio, telling Kim that they were going to playtime pizza restaurant Chuck E. Cheese's. Kim was, as might be expected, stunned to hear her daughter's voice in a song that gleefully predicted her own murder. Eminem has admitted that the song became a "topic of discussion" between him and Kim. "When Kim found out I used our daughter to write a song about killing her, she just blew. We'd split, and we had just got back together for a couple weeks. Then I played her the song and she bugged out."[49]

But Eminem refused to make apologies for working his violent fantasies about his wife into a song. He insisted that the song was not meant to be taken seriously.

> The song is a joke. Kim had been trying to keep me from Hailie and this was to get back at her. It's better to say it on a record than to go out and do it. When Hailie gets old enough, I'll explain to her that Mommy and Daddy weren't getting along at the time. None of it was to be taken literally.[50]

Eminem also claimed that he hadn't had any intention of the song reaching such a wide audience when he wrote it. "I didn't write the song thinking I was going to get a record deal and the song would be huge, or even talked about. I mean, at the most I thought it would be talked about in Detroit, but I didn't figure I was going to get a deal and go nationwide with it."[51]

Eminem says that Hailie has heard "97 Bonnie & Clyde" but is too young to understand what the song is really about.

The Slim Shady LP also includes a song called "Role Model," in which Eminem raps about his immoral behavior and how young people are sure to look up to him. "To me, it's just a record," Eminem says. "The message behind it was just complete sarcasm. I wanted to be clear: Don't look at me like I'm a . . . role model."[52]

The Slim Shady LP sparked protests by feminist groups, conservative politicians, and media commentators. The two most common complaints about Eminem's lyrics were that they were homophobic and that they were disrespectful to women.

Homophobic or Satirical?

Eminem was not afraid of using slurs against homosexuals on *The Slim Shady LP*, and he says several hateful things about "fags." When the album was released, gay and lesbian groups were not impressed, and Eminem gained a reputation as a homophobe. During an interview in Detroit, MTV's Kurt Loder asked Eminem whether he was homophobic. "At first I didn't understand where he got that impression from," Eminem recalled. "I was shocked cause it was the first time I heard it. 'Homophobic?' I even asked. 'Where did you get that from?'"[53]

Loder was referring to a lyric on the track "My Name Is" that implies that one of Eminem's high school teachers made a pass at him. "To me there was nothing homophobic about that line," Eminem says. "It was just a line! It was just something funny, but like most of my lyrics, it got analyzed too much."[54]

Eminem has also defended his use of the word *faggot* on *The Slim Shady LP:* "Faggot to me doesn't necessarily mean 'gay person.' It means a sissy, a man behaving like a girl. If you're battling another dude in a freestyle battle, calling him a faggot, you're chopping down his manhood."[55] But gay and lesbian journalists weren't satisfied with Eminem's disclaimers. In fact, Eminem's behavior led *Gay & Lesbian Review Worldwide* to hypothesize that homophobia is more acceptable than racism:

> In an interview, *Rolling Stone* asked Eminem, "Would you say 'nigger' on a record?" The rapper's response was "that word is not even in my vocabulary. I don't think you can put race alongside gender, a man preferring a man." Here,

Protesters rally against Eminem outside of the Grammy Awards in 2001. Eminem's critics decry the violence and bigotry glamorized in his lyrics.

then, are some of Eminem's words, with "faggot" and "lez" changed to racist and ethnic slurs:

> My words are like a dagger with a jagged edge
> They'll stab you in the head
> Whether you're a nigger or a kike
> Or the chink, wop or wetback
> Pants or dress—hate niggers, the answer is yes. . . .

If Eminem were to put this on an album, he would be attacked, vilified, and disgraced. And yet, when he uses the words "faggot" and "lez"—or "bitch" or "slut," for that matter—it's called humorous and satirical.[56]

While Eminem appeared to dismiss his use of terms that are offensive to gays and lesbians, he continued to insist that he was not homophobic himself. "I don't hate gay people," he insists in a collection of his lyrics with commentary on his songs, *Angry Blonde*, "I just don't stray that way. That's not me, I don't care about gay people. Just don't bring that [stuff] around me."[57]

Antiwomen?

Another element to cause controversy about *The Slim Shady LP* was the way Eminem rapped about women: in particular, he attacked his wife, Kim, and his mother, Debbie Mathers-Briggs. Some critics saw Eminem's attacks on his mother as his attempt to create a kind of hard-luck story to rage against in his music. "Hip-hop's fire is often fueled by drawing on the black community's history of resistance to oppression," noted Christopher John Farley in *Time* magazine. "Since there's not much of a history of

Musical superstar Elton John performs onstage with Eminem in 2001. Gay and lesbian groups claim that many of Eminem's lyrics are staunchly homophobic.

the Man keeping down blond, blue-eyed white kids, Eminem turns to another source to crank up his rage: his mom."[58]

Not every critic was so understanding. In *Insight on the News*, Suzanne Fields wrote:

> Lurking in [Eminem's lyrics] is a cruel depravity that seeks ways to go over the line by singing of macho brutality— of raping women, holding gay men with a knife at their throats and helping a group of friends to take a little sister's virginity. These lyrics are powerful, but the power resides in psychological defensiveness that provides a perverse rationalization for brutality: If you don't love you can't be rejected, so you might as well hate and rape.[59]

But Alan Light of *SPIN* magazine thinks otherwise. "[Eminem] loves women," claims Light, who is considered an Eminem authority. "But he can't handle his disappointment that they're flawed."[60] Eminem's own comments on the matter would seem to support this theory. "I've known [Kim] all my life," he has said. "She's the first true girlfriend I ever had. You grow up with this person, and then they want to leave you. And at first, you don't know what to do."[61]

Eminem also stresses that all of his rages at women are temporary impulses. "The other truth of the matter is, whenever I say something bad about women . . . it usually is an emotion I'm going through at the time."[62]

Critical Reception

Critical reaction to *The Slim Shady LP* was mostly positive, but with a twist. Reviewers tended to recognize Eminem's talent, but they were divided on his subject matter. The *Source* called *The Slim Shady LP* "a place where *Natural Born Killers* meets *Pee Wee's Playhouse*."[63]

Timothy White, the veteran editor of *Billboard* magazine, accused Eminem in an editorial of "making money by exploiting the world's misery."[64] He took the opinion that while Eminem was talented, he was socially irresponsible for rapping demeaning things toward women and homosexuals.

Most critics praised Eminem's talent while questioning the violence and hatred in his lyrics.

Barry Walters of the *Village Voice* said:

> [Eminem is] the most disturbing entertainer I've cared about in years. . . . Eminem most definitely is a knucklehead, but instead of making me angry, he makes me chuckle, wonder, even empathize. Yeah, I think he sometimes goes too far for a snicker or a shock, but that's part of his appeal. When he says he hates himself fifty-seven different ways during the course of the *Slim Shady LP,* I believe him. This loser plays his trailer-trash persona for laughs, but also pathos, and his ability to switch back and forth in the course of a single rhyme is what some people—even I—find upsetting.[65]

USA Today had this to say:

> Much has been made over Eminem's being white, but his real differences from other rappers are more than skin deep. Rather than rapping about the high life, he reflects on hitting "Rock Bottom" or how he might get some payback if he ever had the cash. He admits to being "one sandwich short of a picnic basket," and after hearing him explain to his infant daughter why Mommy is "sleeping" in the trunk of the car, who'd argue?[66]

Alona Wartofsky of the *Washington Post* said, "When Eminem is sticking his raised middle finger up our noses, he's having so much fun that you can't help but laugh—even as you're horrified."[67] And Wendy Case from the *Detroit News* explained, "While his content may seem largely indefensible in the modern age, his skills are indisputable. . . . If you like Eminem, you now have eighteen more reasons to like him. If you don't—he really doesn't care."[68]

Appealing to Kids

One element of Aftermath's marketing campaign for *The Slim Shady LP* that drew criticism from many groups is the way that

Mixed Celebrity Reviews of Eminem

While many celebrities praise Eminem's talent and defend his right to free speech, some are undecided or offended by Eminem's antics. "There are things that I don't understand about what he says," Janet Jackson has stated, as quoted in Hannah Manders's book *Access All Areas: Eminem.* "I guess I'm just as confused as the next person. I'd like to ask him questions myself."

And Manders quotes flamboyant British rocker Boy George saying that he thinks Eminem, or at least the Eminem portrayed in the lyrics of *The Slim Shady LP,* is a brattish, streetwise, emotionally insecure, paranoid child pretending to be a grown-up. Apparently willing to bait Eminem, Boy George claims, "Any man or woman who craves fame is often slightly in love with themselves. Eminem is just another homo-erotic icon in denial."

Eminem's music was aggressively marketed to teenagers, in spite of the frank violence, sex, and anger in his lyrics. Aftermath had Eminem record a family-friendly video for the single "My Name Is" that portrayed Eminem as a loveable prankster, doing impressions and bouncing around the television screen like an energetic clown. For this video, and for radio play, Aftermath released a new, edited version of "My Name Is" with toned-down lyrics. This single, combined with the fun, prank-loving Eminem that was portrayed in the video, convinced many parents that *The Slim Shady LP* was appropriate for children. Once the CD was unwrapped, however, parents all over America were stunned by the actual, unedited lyrics.

"My Name Is" was not the only song from *The Slim Shady LP* to be cleaned up for a radio- and video-friendly version. "Guilty Conscience," a song that describes the death of a drug addict from hallucinogenic mushrooms, was transformed into a song about a girl dying of an allergic reaction to the mushrooms on her pizza.

According to *Rolling Stone,* "For anyone expecting more of the naughty pop-culture-obsessed blonde kid in the clean version of 'My Name Is,' proffered on MTV, *The Slim Shady LP* is some bad-trip netherworld."[69] Many parents, feeling that they had been duped by the kid-friendly image of Eminem that was in constant rotation on MTV, agreed.

Eminem has claimed to be unconcerned about the impressionability of his young fans: "You can't control who likes you. If I got Backstreet Boys fans what am I supposed to do? Turn them away? Whoever likes my stuff, likes my stuff. But just know Slim Shady is hip-hop. I grew up on hip-hop, it's the music I love and it's the music I respect. I respect the culture; that's me."[70]

Eminem has defended himself by pointing out that he never claimed to be a role model and that he is completely honest on his album.

My album isn't for younger kids to hear. It has an advisory sticker and you must be eighteen to get it. That doesn't mean younger kids won't get it, but I'm not responsible for every kid out there. I'm not a role model,

In contrast to the wholesome image of bands like the Backstreet Boys, Eminem has styled himself as a hard-core rapper with no wish to serve as a role model.

and I don't claim to be. I do say things I think will shock people. There's absolutely nothing I wouldn't rap about. I'm a grown man and I speak my mind. I'm not trying to be the next Tupac, but I don't know how long I'm going to be on this planet. So, while I'm here, I might as well make the most of it.[71]

Slim Shady Defends Himself

Eminem has defended the violent fantasies, homophobic language, and misogynistic lyrics on *The Slim Shady LP* in a variety of ways. One of his defenses is that the album is completely autobiographical, and thus every situation on the album is merely repeated from real life.

> My album is so autobiographical that there really shouldn't be any more questions to answer. It's just the story of a white kid who grew up in a black neighborhood and had a pretty bad life. A lot of my rhymes are just to get chuckles out of people. Anybody with half a brain is going to be able to tell when I'm joking and when I'm serious.[72]

Eminem also says that his album is completely honest, whereas perhaps others have the same thoughts but simply don't express them. "I'm not alone in feeling the way I feel. I believe that a lot of people can relate to my [stuff]—whether white, black, it doesn't matter. Everybody gets to the point of 'I don't give a [care].'"[73]

These kinds of strong emotions, Eminem says, are transitory. Often the things one might hear in his lyrics are just spoken in the passion of the moment. His lyrics don't necessarily mean that he feels that way in general—it's merely something that he was thinking while he was upset. "If I'm mad at my girl, I'm gonna sit down and write the most misogynistic . . . rhyme in the world. It's not how I feel in general, it's how I feel at the moment."[74]

But these explanations aside, Eminem admits that he gets great satisfaction out of provoking outrage in others: "Half of the satisfaction I get from releasing music comes from the look on people's faces when they hear it."[75]

Celebrity Support of Eminem

Important names from every part of the music industry have spoken up in defense of Eminem, whether it be his right to free speech or the talent that many performers feel is undeniable.

Madonna, herself quite familiar with controversy in the face of public opinion, says, "He's stirring things up, he's provoking a discussion, he's making people's blood boil. That's what art is supposed to do. Thank God he's rebellious and not well-groomed."[76]

Elton John, the legendary and publicly gay rock-and-roll performer who would later take part in his own Eminem controversy by performing with Eminem at the MTV Video Music Awards, says: "Eminem's music is really hardcore, but it's intelligent, hardcore stuff. It's funny, it's clever, it's poetry and it's musically interesting. Rock and roll has always been about pushing buttons. I've met him and I can say that he's absolutely not homophobic."[77]

Shock rocker Marilyn Manson, a controversial figure himself, says: "Eminem is an exception when it comes to rap and his album will play an important role in the right to free speech. I think he's not afraid to tell anyone and everyone to [bug] off and I like and respect him for that."[78]

Former Beatle Paul McCartney has said that he is impressed by Eminem's talent and wit. "I like some of the Eminem stuff because it's kind of clever. I like the rhythm—I like the attitude and I can imagine if I was a young kid now I'd like that."[79]

Hip-hop/R & B star Missy Elliot is also a big fan of Eminem. "I love him 'cause he's white and he knows he's white. He's just him, and whatever he raps about is what he's going through. I ain't mad at that. He's a successful rapper and a star, whether people want to accept his lyrics or not. He's major."[80]

Comparisons to Elvis

In many ways, Eminem reminded journalists and critics of another white musician who took over a traditionally black form of music and caused a great deal of controversy in the process: Elvis Presley. The *New York Times* has said:

> If there's a particular template for Eminem's career at this
> early point, it's that of the young Elvis (a comparison that

No stranger to controversy herself, Madonna has voiced support for Eminem. Several other famous celebrities have expressed appreciation for the rapper's music.

Eminem hates). Both men took a popular music form invented by African-Americans and gave it a white face. But Eminem has advantages Elvis did not. He writes his own material rather than singing anyone else's songs. His mentor isn't a white impresario like Elvis's manager Colonel Parker, but the legendary hip-hop producer Dr. Dre, whose endorsement gave him instant credibility with black

Eminem and Elvis Presley both fused predominately African American musical styles with their own original styles to create successful recordings.

and white audiences alike and shielded him from accusations of cultural theft.[81]

Jimmy Iovine, the owner of Interscope, views the comparisons to Elvis in a positive light. "I think there's a comparison in the way Elvis fused things. Eminem is very true to hip-hop but does bring some more rock 'n' roll sensibility to it. That's why people respond to it, because in the end, Eminem is really good."[82]

Controversy or no, there's no denying that *The Slim Shady LP* met with huge success and catapulted Eminem to stardom. Eminem's career was finally on the fast track. But his personal life was another story.

Chapter 4

Professional Success, Personal Failures

THE RELEASE OF *The Slim Shady LP* had made the world aware of Eminem's talent, and his celebrity was certainly on the rise. In 1999, Eminem rode a wave of success brought on by the performance of his first album for Aftermath. But in his personal life, Eminem continued to struggle.

Becoming the Biggest Name in Rap

In the wake of *The Slim Shady LP*'s release, Eminem was the most talked-about name in rap, and one of the most infamous names in music in general. Critics, disc jockeys, and other celebrities all crowded around the newly famous rapper, wanting some connection to rap's wonder child. On March 13, 1999, the mayor of Detroit joined the Eminem party, awarding Eminem the key to the city of Detroit. Eminem, perhaps understandably, was finding it all a little hard to believe. "It's good to be home," he stated after the event. "But it's crazy—it's like something you want to happen but never think will."[83]

The amazing sales of *The Slim Shady LP* also led Interscope to send Eminem out on tour. *The Slim Shady LP* tour opened in Chicago, Illinois, on April 7, 1999. It comprised performances in twenty cities, most of them sold out. After the *Slim Shady LP* tour was completed, Eminem joined the Vans Warped tour, a tour of several different artists, as a late replacement for Cypress Hill. After the Vans Warped tour wrapped up, Interscope sent Eminem across the Atlantic to perform in Norway, Sweden, Germany, Austria, Switzerland, the United Kingdom, and the

Netherlands. The European tour, while exhausting, proved to be a great success.

To many, Eminem's sudden arrival on the pop music scene and his unbelievable album sales seemed like overnight success. But Eminem knew how long he had been working toward this goal. "I dealt with a lot of [stuff] coming up, a lot of [stuff]," he has said. "When it's like that, you learn to live day by day. When all this [success] happened, I took a deep breath, just like, 'I did it.'"[84]

Staying Humble

After the release of *The Slim Shady LP*, Eminem's personal life didn't undergo a drastic transformation. In fact, Eminem seemed to make a concerted effort to remain humble, settling in the same neighborhood he grew up in and taking care of his childhood friends.

After *The Slim Shady LP* went double platinum, Eminem still lived with Kim and Hailie in his mother's trailer in a Detroit trailer park. Eminem took over the lease on the trailer when his mother moved back to Kansas City.

Eminem never forgot the friends that he spent most of his time with during his struggling years, the members of D-12. In September 1999, Eminem and Paul Rosenberg launched Shady Records, a label under Aftermath. D-12 was Shady Records' first signing.

Eminem believed it was his responsibility to take care of his old friends. "The same friends I had back then are the same people on tour with me now," he said. "I don't want them to be poor."[85]

Trouble

On September 10, 1999, Eminem's personal life took a difficult turn. Debbie Mathers-Briggs filed suit against Eminem for defamation of character in Mount Clemens, Michigan. Mathers-Briggs claimed that she'd suffered distress, humiliation, and anxiety stemming from his derogatory remarks. She sought $10 million in damages.

Eminem's mother's suit cited several lyrics on Eminem's *The Slim Shady LP*, including his assertion that "my mom does more dope than I do" on the track "My Name Is." She also cited

Surrounded by his entourage, Eminem accepts the award for Best Rap Album of the Year at the 2003 Grammy Awards.

comments made in *Rolling Stone, Rap Pages,* the *Source,* and on the *Howard Stern Show.* She also claimed that while Eminem agreed to take over the mortgage on her trailer in Detroit, he stopped making the payments, and she was evicted.

There's no denying that over the years, Eminem has had many choice words to say about his mother. In *Rolling Stone,* Eminem had claimed that "My mother did a lot of dope and [stuff]—a lot of pills—so she had mood swings. She'd go to bed cool, then wake up like, ' . . . Get out!'"[86]

Eminem has also claimed:

As soon as I turned fifteen, my mother told me "Get a job and help me pay these bills or your [butt] is out." Then she would just kick me out anyway—half the time, right after she took most of my paycheck. . . . My mother is crazy. When I went on tour for the first time, she even took my posters I'd left behind and auctioned them off to the kids in the neighborhood.[87]

Eminem also says that at one of his shows in Kansas City, his mother charged fans twenty dollars to have their picture taken with her son, without telling Eminem. "My mother is a snake,"[88] he says. Eminem has even claimed that his mother keeps him from his half brother, Nathan. When he phones Nathan, Eminem claims his mother listens in. "I'm sure he's afraid of my mother, and I'm sure she's doing the same things to him as she did to me,"[89] he says. For Mathers-Briggs's part, she seems to believe that Eminem's derogatory comments are just part of a larger effort to bolster his hard-luck hip-hop image. "A friend told me, 'Debbie, he's

Eminem's Mom Tries to "Set the Record Straight"

In late 2000, Eminem's very public feud with his mother took a bizarre turn. Debbie Mathers-Briggs released a hip-hop single of her own titled "Set the Record Straight." The single was recorded in collaboration with ID-X rapper Lamar Weeden and singer Jerome Frost and produced by R.E.M. and Indigo Girls collaborator John Keane. Lyrically, "Set the Record Straight" set out to do just that, with Mathers-Briggs attempting to tell her version of Eminem's childhood and insisting that Eminem had gone too far with his lies about her bad mothering. She also claimed that she still loved Eminem and would be there for him when all of this was over. To promote the record, Mathers-Briggs even set up a website, www.marshallsmom.com, which featured streaming audio files of the track and its B-side recordings, and a gallery of pictures from Eminem's childhood. Mathers-Briggs discussed the single in an interview with Amy Reiter, "A Conversation with Eminem's Mom," posted on Salon.com on February 21, 2001:

> I do love my son and I'm not a bad person and it's really difficult. The song, the letter "Dear Marshall," was written for him to basically let him know, "Yes, I do love you." I know he's going through a very stressful time in his life. He has been for two years and I know everything kinda hit him at once with his fame and all that....The message from me is that I love him and I'm not this evil beast that has been portrayed by the media. Like he said, "Mom, it's been the media doing the most harm." I know that. The CD basically is to set the record straight.

saying this stuff for publicity.' He was always well provided for,"[90] she told *Rolling Stone.*

Mathers-Briggs has even hypothesized that she brought this abuse on herself, by sheltering young Marshall. "I sheltered him too much, and I think there's a little resentment from that. People told me I'd be sorry some day. I've never done drugs. Marshall was raised in a drug and alcohol free environment."[91]

Fred Gibson, Mathers-Briggs's lawyer, also suggests that Eminem is using his mother to create a hip-hop-friendly image.

> He's a hip-hop artist, like Vanilla Ice. Vanilla Ice went away a few years ago when it became clear his hard past was a fabrication. This isn't the same, but hip-hop is an urban culture and Eminem is Caucasian. He doesn't fit in, so he has to project this image.[92]

At the time the suit was brought against him, Eminem couldn't comment for legal reasons, and he found that frustrating. "It really pisses me off that I can't talk about it. It gets under my skin a little bit that I can't say things and make comments, because I want to, but I'll just keep quiet right now because I'm paying out my [butt] for lawyers as it is."[93]

Paul Rosenberg, Eminem's manager, claimed that Eminem's defense would simply be that everything he had claimed about his mother was true. "Eminem's life is reflected in his music. Everything he said can be verified as true. Truth is an absolute defense to a claim of defamation."[94]

On November 15, 1999, Rosenberg filed suit to dismiss Debbie Mathers-Briggs's lawsuit, saying it was insufficiently detailed. But Eminem seemed eager for the case to go to trial. "I'd like to watch her put herself in court and make herself look ridiculous," he said at the time. "My own mother suing me is just disgusting. She's just grasping at straws."[95]

In June 1999, Eminem and Kim finally decided to marry, but the wedding was bittersweet as their relationship was still turbulent. One of Eminem's closest friends, DJ Proof, recalls,

> One time we came home and Kim had thrown all his clothes on the lawn–which was, like, two pairs of pants

and some gym shoes. So we stayed at my grandmother's, and Em's like, "I'm leaving her; I'm never going back." Next day, he's back with her. The love they got is so genuine, it's ridiculous. But there's always gonna be conflict there.[96]

To make matters worse, Eminem quarreled with one of the few allies he had left in his family—his grandmother, Betty Kresdin—in late 1999. He asked her for permission to sample an old tape of his beloved Uncle Ronnie rapping on one of the tracks for his new album. Kresdin initially agreed but then changed her mind, and Eminem became furious. "I let the public decide for themselves what idiots my family are," he said at the time. "They've never been there for me. They expect things just because we're blood."[97]

Betty Kresdin wasn't sure what to make of her grandson's angry behavior. "Marshall has changed for the worse. He talks filthy to me and is angry and disrespectful. I don't know what's gotten into him. He's a bitter boy with sad songs who wants to make fame, but Ronnie was a godly person."[98]

Ironically, Kresdin had been one of Eminem's strongest supporters in the lawsuit brought by his mother. "That boy has always had it rough," she claimed. "I admire him for surviving and thriving despite it all."[99]

At this time, Eminem was reportedly indulging in alcohol and drugs more and more in preparation for his next album. It was rumored that Eminem went on a five-day writing binge in Amsterdam after sampling some marijuana and hallucinogens, which are legal in the Netherlands, resulting in five new songs.

Eminem was also rumored to be taking part in some collaborations at this time that never came to be released. Eminem recorded with Limp Bizkit, another Interscope artist, but the song was never released. Eminem also reportedly planned to collaborate with Marilyn Manson on a song called "B— So Wrong," a sequel to "97 Bonnie & Clyde." But according to rumors, Manson took offense at his portrayal on Eminem's "My Name Is" video and backed out of the song.

Shock-rocker Marilyn Manson reportedly backed out of a collaboration with Eminem after taking offense at one of the rapper's videos.

Back into the Studio

In November 1999, Eminem went back into the studio to record his third album, *The Marshall Mathers LP*. He said, "The last album opened you up to Slim Shady's world, and how messed up it is. The next one's going to go more in depth and show you why I got this way."[100] Eminem also claims that he "played with the mic more on *The Marshall Mathers LP*,"[101] creating new sounds and effects.

Eminem now had three distinct public images: Eminem, Slim Shady, and Marshall Mathers. Here's how he shed some light on the differences between the three:

> I'm Marshall Mathers before I'm anything. Marshall Mathers is a regular person, Eminem is a nice guy, and Slim Shady is a [jerk]. Which one do I want for a friend? Marshall. Which one do I most admire? Slim Shady. Who'd win in a fight? Slim Shady. Who's the smartest? Eminem. Who's the loser? Marshall. Who's the winner? Slim Shady.[102]

Public anticipation for Eminem's follow-up to *The Slim Shady LP* was so high, a few tracks leaked out from the studio onto the Internet file-swapping service Napster. A bootleg CD of *The Marshall Mathers LP* tracks was also circulated in the rap scene before the actual CD was released. Dr. Dre and Eminem were upset by these leaks. After that, Aftermath employees were banned from taking tapes out of the studio building.

Grammies

In 2000, Eminem won two Grammies for his work on *The Slim Shady LP*, for best rap album and for outstanding rap solo performance. But Eminem didn't attend the Grammies to receive his awards; he claimed he was too busy working on *The Marshall Mathers LP*. His manager, Paul Rosenberg, claims: "He didn't believe he'd win anything, so he thought his time would be better spent in the studio. He's happy about winning, but these things don't affect him like normal people."[103]

As the early months of 2000 slipped by, Eminem was at a crucial point in his career. Would *The Marshall Mathers LP* retain his place at the top of the rap world? Could it possibly live up to the success of *The Slim Shady LP*?

Chapter 5

Marshall Mathers Takes No Prisoners

THE FOLLOW-UP TO a widely praised and multiplatinum album is always a crucial testing point for musicians. Will the second album live up to the praise and hype of the first? Will the artist retain the talent and vision that made him unique on the first successful album? As summer 2000 approached, many critics and fans wondered whether Eminem would tone down his controversial image to appeal to the masses. But with the follow-up to his multiplatinum album *The Slim Shady LP*, Eminem didn't back away from the anger and controversial topics that made him such a loved and hated figure.

The Marshall Mathers LP was released on May 23, 2000. It sold an amazing 1.7 million copies in its first week of release, going platinum in just seven days. It was clear that Eminem's fans were not going anywhere; if anything, the anticipation for Eminem's next album had gained him new fans. *The Marshall Mathers LP* entered the Billboard top-selling chart at number one, a rare feat even for established musicians.

Still Angry

Many critics wondered whether Eminem could sustain the same level of anger and shocking lyrics on his follow-up to *The Slim Shady LP*. *The Marshall Mathers LP* proved that Eminem still felt all of that anger, and then some. In the track "The Real Slim Shady," Eminem even claims to have killed his mentor, Dr. Dre, and locked his body in the basement. The video for "The Real Slim Shady" embraced this image, even showing a milk carton with the "missing" Dr. Dre's face on it.

The Marshall Mathers LP

☐ Released on May 23, 2000

☐ Entered Billboard charts as the number one best-selling album in America

☐ Sold 1.7 million copies in the first week

☐ Its sales reached platinum in just seven days

Another song on *The Marshall Mathers LP* to encounter controversy was "Stan," a song that depicts an obsessed fan of Eminem's killing his pregnant wife and stuffing her body into the trunk of their car. In the song, Stan writes numerous letters to Eminem, becoming angrier and more unhinged as months go by without response. In the last verse, Eminem finally writes back to Stan, realizing midway through his letter that Stan is the man he saw on the news who killed his pregnant wife. The song is harrowing but also has traces of Eminem's trademark rough humor. Eminem claims that the song was inspired by several obsessed fans he's encountered in his life as a celebrity: "Obviously it's meant to be a joke but this guy was really crazy, took my music seriously and thought he could relate to me. Since I got famous, I do attract loads of weirdos. I've had dudes crying, trying to kiss my hand, and looking at me like I'm some kind of god."[104]

"The Way I Am" is a song that discusses Eminem's stress and fears of failure as he began to write songs for *The Marshall Mathers LP*. As he describes it, "The label was stressing me for a first single for the album. I was feeling the frustration and pressure of trying to top "My Name Is." . . . So I just let it out. The song was a message to the label—to everybody—to just get off my back."[105]

But perhaps the most infamous song on *The Marshall Mathers LP* is "Kim," a prequel to "97 Bonnie & Clyde." In this song, Eminem whispers sweetly to Hailie and then beats Kim, forces her into their car, drives to a remote spot, and strangles her. Eminem says, "This was the hardest song to write because it took every bit of rage that was in me to put it on paper. My music is my therapy. It keeps me partially sane."[106]

Eminem has also claimed that he wrote the song on drugs: "I wrote that [song] while I was on Ecstasy. Ecstasy amplifies whatever mood you're in—love or hatred. I've wanted to kill people on Ecstasy. And then I've had times when I've been telling people I don't know, 'I love you man!'"[107]

Dr. Dre says he respects Kim for staying with Eminem after she heard the song. "If I was her, I would have ran when I heard that [song]. It's over the top—the whole song is him screaming. It's good, though. Kim gives him a concept."[108] According to Eminem, Kim reacted to the song with remarkable tolerance. "Kim listened to ['Kim'], and she just said to me 'You really are crazy.' She doesn't want to listen to the song anymore, and nor do I now. But that song is like an outtake from one of our arguments in everyday life. That's really how we fight sometimes."[109]

But along with the shocking level of anger in the lyrics of "Kim" is a degree of vulnerability. In the song, Eminem asks why Kim doesn't like him and insists that she must think he's ugly, even though she denies it. While "Kim" is undeniably violent, it offers some insight into a complicated relationship.

Dissing Celebrities

On *The Marshall Mathers LP*, Eminem discovered yet another way to shock and provoke: he insulted several celebrities in his lyrics, for various reasons. One of the victims was Will Smith, the actor and rapper who gained fame on the sitcom *The Fresh Prince of Bel Air*. According to Eminem, he became angry when he read a quote from Smith insisting that he would never use foul language in his raps. "I felt Will Smith was taking a stab at me and Dre and anybody else who uses profanity on a record to express themselves."[110]

Teen queen Christina Aguilera was another celebrity who apparently angered Eminem over the course of 1999, and she, too, was dissed on *The Marshall Mathers LP*. Eminem implied in one of his lyrics that Aguilera had engaged in lewd acts with MTV's Carson Daly and Limp Bizkit. In an interview with MTV's Kurt Loder, Eminem indirectly admitted that the accusation wasn't true. But he defended his attack, explaining,

> She heard a rumor that I was married, and then she said [on an MTV special], "He's cute. But isn't he married, though?" And then she said, "Doesn't he have a song about killing his baby's mother?" . . . So I figured, "All right, you said something about me, I'm gonna voice some rumors that I heard about you."[111]

Aguilera was not amused by the attack. She responded: "I just find what he has to say disgusting and just totally untrue. . . . For

Offended by a quote from Will Smith, Eminem insulted the rapper and actor on one of the songs of The Marshall Mathers LP.

whatever reason it seems Eminem has such animosity towards me. I don't know what I said to disturb him, but whatever I said, I'd say it again."[112]

Eminem also attacked a Detroit rap group called Insane Clown Posse. He explained,

> There's a couple of phony white rappers, the Insane Clown Posse. Since I'm white they want to try and take shots at me. I don't like them because they're wack and so they don't like me back. But they're garbage. One of them said something about my daughter, and when I see him, it'll be ugly. Very ugly.[113]

Finally, Eminem frequently dissed the pop world in general, particularly teenybopper acts like Britney Spears, the Backstreet Boys, and *N'SYNC. He explains, "The whole pop world is corny. I just think it's sissy music. It's so watered-down, man. It's like, how many times can you rhyme 'tearin' me apart' and 'breakin' my heart' and 'love, sent from up above.' It's ridiculous, it's repetitive, and it gets on my nerves."[114] But while Eminem angered many of the celebrities he insulted in his lyrics, as usual, he insisted that his remarks were not meant to be taken seriously. "A lot of things I say are not meant to be disses, they're just meant to be me speaking my mind. If I wanna dis somebody, then I'll dis 'em; I'll just come out and say, 'Will Smith, [forget] him.'"[115]

Reviews

Reviews for *The Marshall Mathers LP* were even more positive than for *The Slim Shady LP*. Reviewers spent much more time rhapsodizing about Eminem's talent and less time questioning the political incorrectness of his lyrics: "Talent will overcome," *Rolling Stone* wrote, "and Em is having the last laugh. His off-the-beat flow, way off-the-beat lyrics and looney-tunes presentation place him in a class by himself."[116]

Entertainment Weekly praised Eminem as "a peerless rap poet with a profound understanding of the power of language."[117] *Details* magazine claimed that "his rhymes sting like a lungful of crack."[118] And *Newsweek* called him "not only the heir to Tupac

Shakur and Notorious B.I.G., [but] the most compelling figure in all of pop music."[119]

But some groups still questioned Eminem's place in youth-driven pop culture, voicing concerns about Eminem's message and whether his angry lyrics deserved praise. GLAAD, the Gay and Lesbian Alliance Against Defamation, released this statement in June 2000:

> The hate and hostility conveyed on [Eminem's] CD has a real effect on real people's lives as it encourages violence against gay men and lesbians. While hate crimes against gay people are on the rise, these epithets (on the album) create even more bias and intolerance toward an entire community. The real danger comes from the artist's fan base of easily-influenced adolescents, who emulate Eminem's dress, mannerisms, words and beliefs.[120]

As usual, Eminem refused to respond to his critics. "At the end of the day," he claimed, "I'm always my own worst critic."[121] Also, he insists that music cannot lead a child to commit a violent act. In fact, he believes that music can make young people stronger.

> I don't think music can make you kill or rape someone any more than a movie is going to make you do something you know is wrong. It can make a 15-year-old kid, who is being picked on by everyone and made to feel worthless, throw up his middle finger and say, "[Forget] you. You don't know who I am." It can help make them respect their individuality, which is what music did for me. If people take anything from my music, it should be motivation to know that anything is possible as long as you keep working at it and don't back down. I didn't have nothin' going for me at school or at home until I found something I loved, which was music, and that changed everything.[122]

More Trouble

On June 3, 2000, Eminem got himself into trouble once again. Eminem and Kim were out in downtown Detroit when Douglas Dail

Many people consider Eminem to be the late rap mogul Notorious B.I.G.'s successor.

of the Insane Clown Posse approached Eminem and the two began arguing. Eminem allegedly pulled a semiautomatic firearm from his car and threatened Dail with it. Later, Dail called the police. The police paid Eminem a visit, interviewed him, and charged him with carrying a concealed weapon and brandishing it in public.

Later that same weekend, Eminem drove to the Hot Rocks Club in Warren, Michigan, because he reportedly heard Kim was there with another man. Allegedly Eminem saw Kim kissing the other man, John Guerra, in the parking lot and pistol-whipped him with a nine-millimeter gun. He was picked up by police and charged with assault and carrying an unlicensed weapon; Kim was accused of disturbing the peace. Guerra sued for twenty-five thousand dollars and claimed that Eminem threatened to kill him.

But perhaps the most terrible thing to happen to Eminem during the summer of 2000 was the suicide attempt of his wife, Kim. Earlier that summer, Eminem had joined the Up in Smoke tour with Dr. Dre, Snoop Dog, and Xzibit. The tour was a huge success. During his act, Eminem would bring a naked inflatable doll onstage and refer to it as "Kim." He then proceeded to beat the doll onstage, usually to huge applause from the audience.

This particular part of the act was cut for the Detroit performance, but reinstated in nearby Auburn Hills, where Kim attended

Battling the Insane Clown Posse

Eminem's feud with the rap group the Insane Clown Posse goes back much further than the incident that led to assault charges in Detroit. Like Eminem, the Insane Clown Posse is made up of white rappers from Detroit. Their rivalry with Eminem dates back to 1995, when both acts were trying to break out of the Detroit rap scene. Reportedly, Eminem was booked to play an event at St. Andrew's Hall, and he printed up and distributed flyers to promote the event. The Insane Clown Posse got their hands on a flyer and were outraged to see their own act's name, supposedly booked to play at the same event. But the ICP had no plans to play at the event and accused Eminem of trying to use their name to sell extra tickets to his events. A rap war ensued, with ICP expressing their resentment on tracks like "Nuttin But a Bitch Thang" and "Slim Anus," and Eminem countering on "Marshall Mathers" from *The Marshall Mathers LP*, calling them "Faggot 2 Dope" and "Silent Gay," and criticizing the ICP for calling Detroit their hometown, when in fact the members lived twenty miles outside the city. But Eminem claims that the rivalry isn't as important to him as it is to the Insane Clown Posse. As quoted in Weiner's *Eminem: Talking*, Eminem shrugs:

> I don't think I take the beef as seriously as they do, because I don't consider them artists. They look at me as an artist. I think they get more uptight about it. I can look at them and laugh. They can't do anything to me. What can they do to me? They have no credibility, no respect, no talent, they have nothing. All they can do is diss me vocally, they can't diss me lyrically. There's nothing they can do to me as far as music goes. I don't take it as seriously as they do and that frustrates them.

the show on July 7. At 11:30 that same night, Kim slashed her
wrists in an apparent suicide attempt. She was rushed to Mt.
Clemens General Hospital, but released the same night. Eminem
chose to stay with the tour.

Eminem's and Kim's relationship was clearly in tatters. Kim
appeared so distraught, she made the very unusual move of writing a letter to the local paper to discuss her relationship with her
husband. In a letter to the *Detroit Free Press*, Kim wrote:

> "My husband came up to Hot Rocks to check up on me.
> If I was to cheat on him, it wouldn't be in a neighbor-
> hood bar where he knows where I am. Had he asked any
> questions before he flew off the handle, he would have
> realized that everyone with me, male and female, were
> only friends."[123]

Eminem responded by discussing the tensions between them
in several interviews. He told the *Detroit Free Press*, "Me and the
missus, we go at it. It's no secret we've had our problems, or that
we're still having them. Once you've brought a child into this
world it makes it that much more complicated, especially when
you don't get along with someone."[124]

Kim too seemed to think that their marriage faced great
challenges:

> Just because my husband is an entertainer doesn't mean
> that our personal business is for everyone's entertain-
> ment purposes. I've always taken his word on things and
> stood by his side. None of his fans really know he's mar-
> ried. Females buy 80% of Marshall's records. A lot of the
> fans are girls, and he's good-looking, so they think they
> stand a chance.[125]

Finally, Eminem and Kim's marriage seemed to break under the pressure. In August 2000, Eminem sued for divorce, seek-
ing joint custody of Hailie. Kim countersued for $10 million for
emotional distress. After a couple of weeks, though, Kim dropped
her suit. The pair agreed to a financial settlement. Kim got custody of Hailie, but Eminem was granted generous access.

A 2002 photograph of Eminem's mansion in Clinton Township, Michigan. Fame and fortune have enabled Eminem to rise well above the poverty of his childhood.

Moving On with Sadness

After Eminem and Kim officially split, Eminem bought a new house, a $1.5 million estate in a gated community in Clinton Township, Michigan, in August 2000. To all outward appearances, Eminem seemed to be moving on, but he seemed to be feeling somewhat melancholy, admitting in interviews that he was beginning to see the downside of fame.

> People ask me, "What would you say to someone that wanted to grow up to be like you?" And I would say not to do it.

Don't grow up to be me. But at the same time, is it really a bad thing to grow up to be like me, to come from the gutter and then become a rap star? Is that necessarily a bad thing?[126]

For the first time, Eminem appeared to be considering just what he was giving up in order to find success as a rap star.

I'm missing the best years of my little girl's life. I'm not seeing her grow up. There's gonna be a time when I have to think, "Yo, do I want this?" If I can't find a balance, I'll have to make a choice. I don't know what's going to happen tomorrow. I'll have to see what happens with the next album. Then maybe I can make a decision.[127]

In early 2001, Eminem had to face the lawsuits that had been filed against him. In February, he pleaded guilty in the Hot Rocks

The Privilege and Price of Fame

Eminem reflected on the pros and cons of his sudden fame in a June 30, 2000, interview in the *Detroit Free Press:*

Nobody really understands the pressures put on me, to always be good, to always be on point. There are so many pressures that go with my job right now. It's crazy. . . . You gotta be careful what you wish for. I always wished and hoped for this. But it's almost turning into more of a nightmare than a dream. . . . Not being able to walk down the street anymore, people not treating me like a normal human being anymore. I miss going to the park and playing basketball. I was never that person who wanted big cars and Benzes. All I really wanted to do was have a career in hip-hop and be successful. . . . People would argue, "You got everything you want. You've got money, you don't have to worry about paying bills." But I can't even go in public anymore. I've got the whole world looking at me. I can't be treated like a regular person anymore.

But there are positives, just in the sense that my little brother's not gonna need anything the rest of his life. . . . My *daughter's* not gonna need anything the rest of her life. Sometimes I feel like I'm living my life for everyone else. I wake up at seven in the morning, and the rest of the day is work. I can't sleep. I don't eat. It's just crazy. It's a lot of . . . work, a lot more work than I ever expected.

case to carrying a concealed weapon. Prosecutors announced that they would seek a jail term at the April sentencing, but Eminem was allowed to go on a European tour anyway. While in England, Eminem was reportedly caught taking narcotics onstage, but he convinced the local police that he was merely eating sweets. On April 10, 2001, Eminem was sentenced to three years' probation—one for the Dail case and two for the Guerra incident. He was also banned from owning firearms. He was fined $2,500, plus $5,000 in court fees, and told to pay $60 to a local crime victims' fund.

In mid-2001, Eminem had proven himself twice over as a rap artist to be reckoned with, but his personal life was falling apart. He had gained acceptance from the music industry in general, but mainstream America still viewed him as controversial and somewhat dangerous. Then Eminem was presented with a very interesting opportunity: could he be a movie star? That opportunity—and the resulting film, *8 Mile*—would dramatically change the course of Eminem's career.

Chapter 6

Going Hollywood

Eminem grew up loving movies, and shortly after the release of *The Marshall Mathers LP*, he was presented with the opportunity to appear in one himself. While he was reluctant to commit to a movie project, *8 Mile*, based loosely on Eminem's own life, brought Eminem critical acclaim as an actor and something even harder to earn: mainstream acceptance.

Eminem, the Movie Star

Actually, Eminem had explored the possibility of acting in in a film long before he agreed to shoot *8 Mile*. He shot four scenes playing himself for director Dale Restighini's direct-to-video horror spoof *Da Hip Hop Witch* in 2000. According to *Entertainment Weekly*, however, Eminem suddenly got cold feet a few months before the film's release and asked to be cut from the film.

But in early 2000, some very important movie-industry people were beginning to wonder about this new rap superstar, Eminem. In his videos, Eminem relayed incredible charisma and the camera loved him. It led producer Brian Grazer, known for films like *How the Grinch Stole Christmas, The Nutty Professor*, and *A Beautiful Mind*, to wonder whether Eminem might be able to translate that charisma to the movie screen.

According to Eminem's manager, Paul Rosenberg, Grazer wasn't the first to approach Eminem about appearing in a movie, but he had the good fortune to be part of the same parent company as Interscope. "We kept getting offers. From action movies to weird indie flicks to horror movies," says Rosenberg. "But nothing I thought he'd be good at, like a drama or comedy. We were shopping around and [someone] said, 'Talk to Grazer. Give

69

Universal a shot. . . . Because that's our parent company.'"[128]

Eminem agreed to attend a meeting with Grazer, but according to sources, it didn't go particularly well. Eminem sat in complete silence for fifteen minutes, refusing to even look at Grazer. "His indifference to me, to Hollywood, were palpable,"[129] Grazer says:

> Even though [*The Marshall Mathers LP*] hadn't dropped yet and he wasn't even that big a star, he would not even look at me. He just stared straight ahead for about fifteen minutes. I went in the bathroom and I looked at myself in the mirror and was like, "Is this guy ever gonna talk to me?"[130]

Eventually Eminem did start talking, and Grazer was able to convince him of something that Grazer himself was already sure of–Eminem had movie-star quality, "the ability to find some part of themselves in anything they play."[131] After an awkward conversation recalling his childhood and his experiences in the rap world, Eminem finally agreed to work on a movie project with Grazer's studio, Universal. It was agreed that Dr. Dre would have the chance to review and approve everything, to give the project hip-hop credibility. Grazer suggested Scott Silver, a screenwriter who had been struggling ever since cowriting the 1999 flop *The Mod Squad*, to write the screenplay. Eminem agreed, and Silver was sent to tag along with Eminem on the Up in Smoke tour, absorb as much of the rap world and Eminem's personality as he could, and come back with a script for a dramatic movie.

The resulting script was *8 Mile*, originally called *Fight Music*. It was loosely based on Eminem's life, and it portrayed the struggles of a white rapper from Detroit, Jimmy "Rabbit" Smith Jr., as he tried to make it in freestyle rap battles while dealing with his childish, substance-abusing mother and trying to raise his younger sister. The script was approved by Dr. Dre and the studio, and the studio tapped *L.A. Confidential* director Curtis Hanson to direct the movie. Hanson spent some time with Eminem in Detroit and came away convinced that he and Eminem would work well together. Hanson's team was not quite so convinced, as he recalled to *Entertainment Weekly:*

Eminem arrives at the 2002 premiere of his movie, 8 Mile. The rap star made a successful transition from the recording studio to the movie set.

There was some, um, questioning from my agents about working with someone so controversial. But I'm old enough to have witnessed the ways in which Lenny Bruce and Richard Pryor were misunderstood and taken out of context, so I'm sensitive to [his situation].[132]

Eminem was also confident that he and Hanson would make a good team. He says of Hanson,

I had seen [Hanson's movie] *The Hand That Rocks the Cradle*. But people kept telling me about *L.A. Confidential* and so I watched it. Three times. I was like, damn! 'Cause it was a good movie and there was [stuff] that I didn't get until the third time. That's when I knew, yo, this guy isn't playing.[133]

With a director in place, Universal began casting the parts of Rabbit's mother and would-be girlfriend. *L.A. Confidential* actress Kim Basinger was cast as Rabbit's mother, and up-and-coming young actress Brittany Murphy, who had appeared in *Don't Say a Word* and *Girl, Interrupted*, was cast as Rabbit's love interest. Murphy admits that she was nervous about meeting

Kim Basinger outside the Los Angeles premiere of 8 Mile *in 2002. The actress portrays Eminem's mother in the movie.*

Eminem. "I was about to meet this force of nature," Murphy recalls. "But we had just gone through something huge [*8 Mile* rehearsals began just days after the attacks on the World Trade Center on September 11, 2001], so I wasn't gooey star-struck. I saw the bigger picture."[134]

Eminem had great respect for his fellow actors and got along well with Basinger and Murphy. He got on so well with Murphy, in fact, that they were rumored to be romantically involved for the duration of the shoot.

Acting was a challenge for Eminem, but according to his comments, it was a challenge that he enjoyed. He recalls,

> At first I thought [acting] was going to be easy. I actually said that! [Curtis and I] had a conversation in my driveway and I said, "I don't think there's going to be anything to this acting thing. Once I can focus on something and just give it 100 percent, I won't let you down." And he laughed and was like, "Marshall, I'm going to tell you like this, it's not as easy as it looks." When I started going through the rehearsals I started realizing . . . [the rehearsals were] grueling.[135]

And for Eminem, he truly was acting. The similarities between Eminem and Rabbit were notable, but "I don't play me in the movie," Eminem told *Rolling Stone*. "There are similarities because I sat down with Scott Silver, the scriptwriter, and told him instances from my life."[136]

According to all sources, filming went well. Eminem behaved like a consummate professional, and the movie was made with no disruptions.

Marketing Slim Shady to the Mainstream

Once *8 Mile* was in the can, Universal faced an interesting dilemma: how to market Eminem, the controversial and sometimes offensive rap musician, to the mainstream movie audiences that a movie must reach in order to be profitable? How could Universal interest the moms and conservative kids who found Eminem's lyrics objectionable without turning off the hard-core rap fans who had followed his career thus far? According to *Advertising Age*, the challenge faced by Universal was in "delicately marketing a huge music star to a broader consumer market, all without harming his core audience."[137]

The studio began by creating a "buzz" marketing campaign. They placed posters in selected cities that featured Eminem and the words *8 Mile*, but no further information. The goal was to get people talking about Eminem's *8 Mile* project, what it might be, and when it might be coming out.

The studio then began to try to make the mainstream audience view Eminem in a new light. The studio created an offbeat trailer for *8 Mile*, which opened with someone singing a soothing lullaby; after a few verses, it is revealed that the singer is none other than the hard-talking rapper, Eminem. "He was singing to his sister [in the movie]," says a Universal rep. "This was surprising and hopefully had people saying, 'Maybe I need to rethink what I know about Eminem.'"[138]

The ad campaign appeared to have been successful when *8 Mile* grossed more than $50 million in its first weekend of release. But the studio knew that the movie's staying power would depend on the reviews.

8 Mile Reviews

When good reviews for *8 Mile* began pouring in from mainstream magazines that had very different opinions on Eminem and his music, Universal knew that they had a big movie on their hands.

"Eminem is a screen natural," praised *USA Today*, " in *8 Mile* . . . he does himself proud. Three and a half stars (out of four)."[139] Normally conservative *Time* magazine gushed,

> [Eminem's] acting has the potential to draw in, even enchant people to whom hip-hop has just been a scary blare of rage emanating from the car drawn up next to them at a stop sign. Against their better judgment, they may even respond to the good nature, even the innocence, of this movie, its desire to—well, yes, let's use the deadly word—educate us about a world of scabrous lyrics and occasional murderous violence.[140]

And *Newsweek* proclaimed,

> Movie-wise viewers may recognize Rabbit as a descendant
> of those '30s working class heroes played by Jimmy Cagney
> and John Garfield, soulful tough guys fighting their way out
> of the slums. It's too early to place Eminem beside those
> Hollywood giants, but the promise is there. He understands
> the power of being still in front of a camera. Compact,
> volatile and burningly intense, he's got charisma to spare.[141]

Even the *8 Mile* sound track, for which Eminem wrote and
recorded three new songs, received raves. *Rolling Stone* proclaimed
the new tracks "three of the most ferocious hip-hop songs ever
recorded. In less than fifteen minutes, these three performances
. . . make you forget Slim Shady ever existed."[142]

Eminem's performance even ignited Oscar buzz, although
Eminem would ultimately fail to win a nomination. The enter-
tainment-industry bible, *Variety*, noted,

The Real Slim Shady

E! Online reporter Ted Casablanca asked some of Eminem's costars in *8
Mile* what the biggest misconceptions are about Eminem. Here are some
of their responses, posted November 14, 2002:

Evan Jones: "That he's mean and aggressive. He's not. The guy I met
was a father and a caring guy who invited me over for Thanksgiving."

Taryn Manning: "Probably that he's mean. I remember doing a scene
with him where I was yelling and screaming at him, and I watched
his eyes, and he was really feeling it. I saw a real sensitivity in him.
As if I were really his girlfriend."

Eugene Byrd: "That he doesn't care. That he dislikes gays. That he's
not a nice person. That's he's hard to deal with. None of those things
are true."

Mekhi Phifer: "That he's all hatred and anger. He's an artist, and
what he says expresses himself."

Brittany Murphy: "I'll tell you something people maybe aren't aware
of, as opposed to a misconception—because that would be refor-
mulating ideas people already have. Eminem's an incredible father.
He and his daughter, Hailie Jade, are this dynamic duo. They're un-
beatable, and seeing that is very inspirational. Every spare moment
he spends with that child. He's also funny."

> The Academy elite has to be re-evaluated. . . . What makes
> *8 Mile* accessible to a voting audience that has, to put it
> mildly, not been part of Eminem's fan base, is the story's
> account of Jimmy (Eminem) bucking the odds and prov-
> ing that he can be a rapping heavyweight. The narrative
> fits comfortably inside an old showbiz framework that
> stretches at least as far back as *42nd Street* and, for shorter-
> term memories, *Flashdance.*[143]

While the film would not, in the end, earn major Oscar nomina-
tions, *8 Mile* would go on to become an extremely successful movie
for Universal, raking in box office receipts of more than $115 mil-
lion and breaking DVD sales records in its first day of release, selling more than $40 million worth of copies in one day, the high-
est amount for any R-rated movie.

The Eminem Show

On May 26, 2002, a few months before the release of *8 Mile*,
Eminem released his third album, *The Eminem Show.* The first single, the hip-hop and beat-driven "Without Me," was a fun, one-
liner-rich song about the joys of coming back on the music scene
after two years away. Eminem filmed another fun, kid-friendly
video for the song, which featured him as a sort of comic-book
superhero. In "Without Me," Eminem jokingly boasts that the music world would be a dull and depressing place without him, but
he says that the song was written with a certain degree of honest
fear of being removed from the scene by the legal system, after
his concealed-weapon arrests in 2000.

> I thought I was gonna go away and people was gonna for-
> get. Some artists that go to jail, people forget about them.
> Their name ain't out there. Everything that you've worked
> for . . . I thought everything that I worked for could crum-
> ble, like, any day, you know? So that was nerve-racking.[144]

Other notable songs on the album include "Cleaning Out My
Closet," in which Eminem apologizes to his mother for hurting
her with his comments even as he insists that she was a terrible
mother and deserves his abuse. The video for this song included

Dressing Shady Style

Eminem's distinctive peroxide-blond hair and tattoos have set style trends far beyond rap and hip-hop circles. Now he hopes to further popularize his fashion sense. One of Eminem's many spin-off enterprises following his great success as a rapper is the launch of a trademarked clothing line, Shady Ltd. Expected to hit retailers such as Macy's in July 2004, the Shady Ltd. collection features clothing that represents Eminem's own particular brand of hip-hop style. Oversized hooded sweatshirts and track pants, baggy denim jeans, and logo T-shirts make up the bulk of the Shady Ltd. line. Accessories include baseball caps, sweatbands, and knit caps, all recognizable Eminem apparel. According to the official Shady Ltd. website, "Shady Ltd. represents a collection that reflects urban style. It's about no restrictions, just an attitude that lets you be different and looking good."

Eminem and his extras rehearse for a 2000 MTV Video Music Awards performance.

the creepy image of Eminem digging a grave in the rain as he rapped about his hatred for his mother. "Honestly, there is no relationship with me and my mother," Eminem said at the time the album was released. "There wasn't really one to begin with, but that song is like my closure song."[145]

The album also included "Hailie's Song," a ballad about Eminem's love for his daughter that features the rapper actually crooning; "Say Goodbye Hollywood," in which Eminem questions his decision to "go Hollywood" by becoming a celebrity and appearing in a movie; and "White America," a song in which Eminem

admits that he wouldn't be as successful as he is if he wasn't white.
Eminem viewed the album as a musical step forward:

> I feel like I really matured, and [with] this album, more
> than anything, I wanted to show growth as an artist. In or-
> der for you to stay afloat in this business, you have to ma-
> ture and you have to reinvent yourself, stay fresh.
> Especially with hip-hop. It's so changing forever, and it
> keeps elevating and going onto different levels.[146]

For the most part, reviewers appeared to agree with Eminem.
And for the first time, reviews seemed to concentrate on the talent Eminem displayed on the album, rather than discussing the
offensiveness or shock value of the lyrics. It appeared that, with
time, Eminem's violent and angry lyrics had become old hat. Little
by little, Eminem was gaining mainstream acceptance.
    Rolling Stone rhapsodized about *The Eminem Show*, claiming:

> With *The Eminem Show*, Eminem may just have made the
> best rap-rock album in history. . . . *The Eminem Show* has the
> self-assurance of an artist at the top of his game [who has] the
> understanding that the music world is hanging on his every
> word and the willingness to shock even the most jaded ears.[147]

Entertainment Weekly wasn't quite as impressed, giving the album as
a whole a B+, but they also recognized that *The Eminem Show* seemed
to show a maturing and deepening of Eminem's talent:

> [The most personal songs] are still among the album's most
> penetrating moments. They test him and his audience, who
> may not want to hear sincerity and psychological prob-
> ing. But they also succeed in fleshing out Eminem's com-
> plexities and contradictions. . . . *The Eminem Show* is a tes-
> tament to the skills of its star. The sludgy rapping of such
> guests as D-12 only confirms Eminem's dizzying prowess,
> gob-spewing individuality, and wickedly prankish humor.[148]

As 2002 drew to a close, Eminem was becoming one of the most
bankable and critically respected rap stars in history. With the
world seemingly in the palm of his hand, what could be next?

Chapter 7

Looking Forward

As 2003 OPENED, it was, quite frankly, a good time to be Eminem. His movie, *8 Mile*, was playing to packed houses and generating Oscar buzz. His latest album, *The Eminem Show*, had garnered critical raves and was selling in record numbers. But what was next for the rap-star-turned-actor? With his star burning brighter than ever before, Eminem has some important decisions to make as he faces a future where he's no longer America's bad boy.

Mainstream Acceptance

With the release of *The Eminem Show*, closely followed by the release of *8 Mile*, critics and rap fans noticed something about the

A customer listens to a CD at a music store. In recent years, Eminem's album sales have soared because the rapper has made efforts to endear himself to mainstream America.

controversial figure of Eminem: he didn't seem so controversial anymore. Audiences at the 2002 Anger Management tour looked very different from audiences at Eminem's previous performances. Scattered among the teenage boys were younger boys and girls, often chaperoned by their parents. "It's kind of strange," Eminem admitted. "[The age of my audiences] used to range from 10 years old to 25. Now it seems to be from 5 to 55."[149]

At the same time, many of the rough lyrics on *The Eminem Show*, where Eminem jokingly referred to being in trouble with the government, had gone virtually unnoticed by Washington or protest groups. "It's something that we've blatantly noticed,"[150] Eminem told the *New York Times*. Suddenly, it was okay to be Eminem.

Curtis Hanson, the director of *8 Mile*, hypothesized that Eminem's omnipresence, his cultural familiarity, make him acceptable to mainstream America. "People are accepting Eminem because he's a superstar,"[151] he has said.

It appears that even the U.S. government is satisfied to let Eminem represent America abroad. In summer 2002, government-sponsored broadcasts included some of Eminem's songs as part of a propaganda campaign to improve America's image in the Middle East.

Some of Eminem's observers wonder if this acceptance is such a good thing. *Vibe* music editor Eric Parker says:

> [*8 Mile* established Eminem as] the good guy, an actor to be taken seriously. He was no longer thumbing his nose at authority but became acceptable. This is a title he doesn't want. He's put himself in a position where he's able to sell records to a giant cross section, but what he wants to represent is the cutting edge of urban music. . . . Street credibility is critical. If you ring true with the black urban kids in the cities, you have a chance to stay cool with the suburban white kids who follow.[152]

It's also unclear whether Eminem *wants* to be America's sweetheart, a character that moms and dads are comfortable leaving with their children. For the most part, Eminem has been laying low since the release of *8 Mile*, staying out of the public spotlight.

Perhaps he's trying to avoid becoming overexposed—too familiar to the American mainstream, and too nonthreatening.

Personal Life

Eminem's divorce from Kim became final in October 2001, and they have since maintained an amicable relationship. The same can't be said for Eminem's relationship with his mother, Debbie Mathers-Briggs, whose $11 million defamation suit against the rapper was eventually settled for a mere $1,600. "I'm dead to you," Eminem tells her on *The Eminem Show*.

After his divorce from Kim, Eminem was rumored to be romantically linked with several celebrities: Kim Basinger (both her reps and his deny that they dated), Brittany Murphy (his rep admits to a relationship that had ended by summer 2002; she has responded to queries with "I would like to always respect the one ounce of privacy that he has. I cherished working with him and I cherish him"[153]), and fellow recording artist Mariah Carey. Reportedly, Eminem met with Carey in 2001 to discuss a possible collaboration that didn't work out. Eminem claims that they were involved, but Carey's reps decline to comment. "There's truth to [rumors of a relationship]," Eminem told *Rolling Stone*. "But on the whole personal level, I'm not really feeling it. I just don't like her as a person."[154]

Eminem reconciled briefly with Kim in October 2002. Eminem clearly had a hard time getting through their divorce. "Divorce is the hardest thing I've ever worked through,"[155] he has said. But their reconciliation ended in June 2003, with Kim reportedly becoming angry when she learned that Eminem had used Hailie's voice on a record dissing his rap rival Ja Rule.

Hailie

One aspect of Eminem's life that has never caused him strife or diminished in importance is the presence of his daughter, Hailie Jade. He calls her "the most important thing in my life."[156] Eminem claims that he doesn't swear in her presence. He makes a point to cook her breakfast, watch *Powerpuff Girls* with her, and shower her with presents. "He's one of those sucker daddies,"[157] claims Denaun Porter, a member of D-12.

Singer Mariah Carey is just one of the celebrities with whom Eminem has been rumored to be romantically involved.

Eminem's grandmother, Betty Kresdin, with whom Eminem has reconciled, says "If Hailie wanted a hamburger at one o'clock in the morning, he'd go get it." He's so obsessed with tending to Hailie these days, she says, that "he has no life anymore."[158] And Eminem has reportedly shown the same soft-heartedness to other children. He has reportedly taken in Kim's sister's daughter, who is two years older than Hailie.

Eminem says that his love for Hailie, and his desire to make a good life for her, are the things that keep him going when fame seems like too much to take.

> Much as I hate doing the interviews and the photo shoots and all the extra work that goes with the territory, I do it so my daughter's future is secure. So that when I die, if she never makes anything of herself–God forbid, because I want her to do something, be a model, do music, be a doctor, anything–I'm gonna have that money there for her. I want her future to be set. I make music so that I can be a family with Kim and Hailie and raise my daughter the right way and not cut out like my father did to me. My family is all I have ever fought for and all I've ever tried to protect. The only thing I'm scared of is being taken away from my little girl.[159]

Maturing

According to his neighbors in Clinton Township, Michigan, Eminem is an ideal neighbor, attending community meetings, chatting up residents (who refer to him as Marshall), and inviting the neighbors' kids to play basketball with him and Hailie. "He's a great neighbor," says one resident. "I'd take ten more like him."[160]

According to Eminem, the concealed-weapons and assault cases brought against him in 2000 were a wake-up call. Being forced to behave, as he was put on probation, "was almost a blessing in disguise,"[161] Eminem told the *Los Angeles Times*. He expanded on this idea to mtv.com:

> It was a reality check. It straightened me up and started making me realize, A, to calm down, and B, that this . . .

could all end tomorrow. My worst fear was, "How am I going to explain this to Hailie? What am I gonna say if I'm found guilty and I gotta do a prison sentence?"[162]

Now, Eminem says, he is trying to mature while maintaining the rawness of his lyrics.

I'm always going to be me no matter what. There's always going to be a part of me that's going to be as raw as when I first came out. There's always going to be that part that I can revert to if I want to go back and be that battle M.C. and say those funny punch lines and stuff to make people laugh or make people angry. But as I grow as a person and as I get older I've got to mature. . . . My daughter is growing up, and I'm trying to set an example for her.[163]

Eminem Now

Eminem stands at a remarkable place in his career. *The Eminem Show* was the top-selling album of 2002, and his movie, *8 Mile*, had the biggest debut ever for a first-time leading actor. *The Eminem Show* was also a critical success. Eminem believes that his talent, and not just his ability to shock and offend, have gotten him where he is today. "I wouldn't have gotten anywhere in this business if I was just a complete [jerk],"[164] he says. But his infamous image still seems to be what he is best known for. *Rolling Stone* named him one of its 2002 People of the Year, but not without reservations:

His brutal wit, his energy, his inventive rhyme-slinging are all at a peak. So, unfortunately, are all the things people can't stand about Em: his self-pity, his ego, his pomposity, his thin whine, his . . . terror of women and gay people and everyone else who doesn't fit into his tight-assed little vision of the world.[165]

Rolling Stone went on to cite an incident that took place at the 2002 MTV Video Music Awards, in which Eminem became furious at Triumph the Insult Comic Dog, a hand puppet that is a recurring character on *The Conan O'Brien Show*. "Em had his all-time

Eminem's Feud with Ja Rule

According to Kim Mathers, it wasn't Eminem's raps about Kim that pushed the couple to split again in June 2003—it was the effects of his feud with rival rapper Ja Rule. Kim charges that Eminem endangered their daughter, Hailie, by using Hailie's voice on raps denouncing Ja Rule. On "Hailie's Revenge," only available as an underground mix tape, Eminem reportedly asks Hailie to bring him his Oscar so they can assault Ja Rule with it, and then suggests insultingly that Ja Rule and Hailie are the same size. Kim believes that by using Hailie's voice on the song, Eminem has dragged Hailie into the potentially violent feud between him and Ja Rule, which reportedly began with insulting remarks made by Ja Rule about Eminem's mother, wife, and daughter.

most embarrassing moment as a star this year at the MTV Video Music Awards, when he tried to pick a fight with a hand puppet. Surrounded by bodyguards, trying to bully a piece of mangy brown fabric, Em just looked kinda pathetic." The article concluded, "Eminem, the biggest star—and biggest pain in the ass—of 2002."[166]

Eminem in the Future

Eminem has branched out as a producer, with his Shady Records label backing the albums of 50 Cent (whose first major-release album, *Get Rich or Die Tryin'*, has been incredibly successful) and Obie Trice (who had a cameo role in *8 Mile*). Eminem is also launching a clothing collection, called Shady Ltd. sportswear. And reportedly a line of dolls—yes, dolls—is in the works for Eminem. There are rumored to be two dolls in the line: One, called Marshall Mathers, is to be a straightforward Ken-type doll, following Eminem's features and clothing style. The second, called Slim Shady, is described as an "extreme" version of Marshall Mathers, wielding a chainsaw and wearing a gas mask.

What's next for Eminem? Brian Grazer, the producer who finally convinced Eminem to perform in *8 Mile*, believes that more movies might be in his future:

> It was hard for me to get him to do *8 Mile*, even when the stars and planets had aligned, and there was a great Scott Silver script with a world and a character that he

50 Cent

The first true breakout success to come from Eminem's label, Shady Records, is rapper 50 Cent, a rough-and-tumble rapper from Jamaica, Queens, New York City, whose official website bio at www.50cent.com describes him as "a man of the streets, intimately familiar with its codes and its violence." Signed first to Run-DMC's Jam Master Jay's label, JMJ Records, and then to Columbia, 50 Cent (whose real name is Curtis Jackson) publicizes his violent past. He is best known for the April 2000 incident in which he was shot nine times in front of his grandmother's house in Queens. During his extended recovery time, Columbia dropped him from the label. 50 Cent continued to record and release albums independently, and soon, one of his bootleg CDs caught Eminem's attention. Eminem signed 50 Cent to Shady Records, and collaborated with Dr. Dre to produce 50's first album for Shady, *Get Rich or Die Tryin'*. 50 Cent claims to be thrilled to be working with Eminem and Dr. Dre. "Creatively, what more could I ask for?" he asks jokingly in an interview on his website. "You know if me and Em is in the same room then it's gonna be a friendly competition, neither of us wanna let the other one down. And Dre??? C'mon." *Get Rich or Die Tryin'* peaked at number one on Billboard's Top 100 Albums chart.

Rapper 50 Cent is the first commercial success produced by Eminem's record label, Shady Records.

knew, and a great director to guide him. But once he commits, I think he can master anything he tries to do. He was determined and a perfectionist who was never a minute late. At some point, I'm sure he'll do another movie.[167]

Eminem himself wonders how his own celebrity could get any bigger. "It's a little spooky," he says. "I mean, thinking how many records I've sold and all the things that I've been through, how could I possibly get any bigger? And if I do, how can I deal with that? I don't know."[168]

But Eminem thinks he's got a career plan if this rap thing doesn't work out. "I'd like to think I can keep a lengthy rap career going," he has said. "But if not, I'll just go back to washing dishes."[169]

Whatever happens, one thing is certain: Eminem is *not* going to watch his mouth:

> I'd like to think I don't come across as arrogant or conceited or big-headed or anything like that. It's just me; I come across as Marshall Mathers, somebody who doesn't take [crap] from anybody. I don't know. . . . I'm a real person. I answer all these questions in my music, anything that people were wondering about me. It's all there, everything that anybody needs to know about me.[170]

Eminem will soon be going back into the studio to record his follow-up to *The Eminem Show*. The world awaits another chapter in the Eminem story.

Notes

Chapter 1: Early Hardships

1. Quoted in Charles Aaron, "Chocolate on the Inside," *SPIN*, May 1999.
2. Quoted in Martin Huxley, *Eminem: Crossing the Line.* New York: St. Martin's Griffin, 2000, p. 7.
3. Quoted in Kelly Kenyatta, *You Forgot About Dre: The Unathorized Biography of Dr. Dre and Eminem.* Phoenix, AZ: BUSTA Books, 2001, pp. 89–90.
4. Quoted in Anthony Bozza, "Eminem Blows Up," *Rolling Stone,* April 29, 1999.
5. Quoted in Bozza, "Eminem Blows Up."
6. Quoted in Bozza, "Eminem Blows Up."
7. Quoted in Bozza, "Eminem Blows Up."
8. Quoted in Kenyatta, *You Forgot About Dre*, p. 91.
9. Quoted in Huxley, *Eminem: Crossing the Line*, p. 9.
10. Quoted in Bozza, "Eminem Blows Up."
11. Quoted in Aaron, "Chocolate on the Inside."
12. Quoted in Ian Gittins, *Eminem.* London: Carlton Books, 2001, p. 8.
13. Quoted in Aaron, "Chocolate on the Inside."
14. Quoted in Aaron, "Chocolate on the Inside."
15. Quoted in Huxley, *Eminem: Crossing the Line*, p. 12.
16. Quoted in Kenyatta, *You Forgot About Dre*, p. 92.
17. Quoted in Chuck Weiner, *Eminem: Talking.* London: Omnibus Press, 2002, p. 27.
18. Quoted in Hannah Mander, *Access All Areas: Eminem.* London: Michael O'Mara Books, 2001, p. 32.

19. Quoted in Gittins, *Eminem,* p. 10.
20. Quoted in Huxley, *Eminem: Crossing the Line,* p. 15.
21. Quoted in Gittins, *Eminem,* pp. 10–11.
22. Quoted in Bozza, "Eminem Blows Up."
23. Quoted in Huxley, *Eminem: Crossing the Line,* p. 24.
24. Quoted in Gittins, *Eminem,* p. 21.
25. Quoted in Huxley, *Eminem: Crossing the Line,* pp. 30–31.
26. Quoted in Huxley, *Eminem: Crossing the Line,* p. 16.

Chapter 2: Meet Slim Shady

27. Quoted in Weiner, *Eminem: Talking,* p. 9.
28. Quoted in Gittins, *Eminem,* p. 14.
29. Quoted in Weiner, *Eminem: Talking,* p. 10.
30. Quoted in Huxley, *Eminem: Crossing the Line,* p. 15.
31. Quoted in Gittins, *Eminem,* p. 15.
32. Quoted in Huxley, *Eminem: Crossing the Line,* p. 25.
33. Quoted in Gittins, *Eminem,* p. 16.
34. Quoted in Gittins, *Eminem,* p. 17.
35. Quoted in Kenyatta, *You Forgot About Dre,* p. 98.
36. Quoted in Huxley, *Eminem: Crossing the Line,* p. 33.
37. Quoted in Gittins, *Eminem,* p. 18.
38. Quoted in Gittins, *Eminem,* p. 17.
39. Quoted in Gittins, *Eminem,* p. 18.
40. Quoted in Bozza, "Eminem Blows Up."
41. Quoted in Bozza, "Eminem Blows Up."
42. Quoted in Matt Diehl, "Will the Real Marshall Mathers Please Stand Up?" *CosmoGIRL!,* April 2003, p. 114.
43. Quoted in Aaron, "Chocolate on the Inside."
44. Quoted in Gittins, *Eminem,* p. 17.
45. Quoted in Huxley, *Eminem: Crossing the Line,* p. 37.

Chapter 3: Success and Controversy

46. Quoted in Weiner, *Eminem: Talking,* p. 85.
47. Quoted in Eminem, *The Slim Shady LP,* Interscope Records, 1999.
48. Quoted in Gittins, *Eminem,* p. 21.
49. Quoted in Gittins, *Eminem,* p. 22.

50. Quoted in Gittins, *Eminem*, p. 22.

51. Quoted in Gittins, *Eminem*, p. 23.

52. Quoted in Eminem, *Angry Blonde*. New York: Regan Books, 2002, p. 48.

53. Quoted in Gittins, *Eminem*, p. 25.

54. Quoted in Gittins, *Eminem*, p. 25.

55. Quoted in Gittins, *Eminem*, p. 25.

56. Quoted in Robin Tyler, "Eminem: Pied Piper of Hate," *Gay & Lesbian Review Worldwide*, May 2001.

57. Quoted in Eminem, *Angry Blonde*, p. 4.

58. Quoted in Christopher John Farley, "A Whiter Shade of Pale," *Time*, May 29, 2000.

59. Quoted in Suzanne Fields, "Bad Raps: Music Rebels Revel in Their Thug Life," *Insight on the News*, May 21, 2001.

60. Quoted in Diehl, "Will the Real Marshall Mathers Please Stand Up?"

61. Quoted in Diehl, "Will the Real Marshall Mathers Please Stand Up?"

62. Quoted in Diehl, "Will the Real Marshall Mathers Please Stand Up?"

63. Quoted in Huxley, *Eminem: Crossing the Line*, p. 40.

64. Quoted in Gittins, *Eminem*, p. 24.

65. Quoted in Huxley, *Eminem: Crossing the Line*, p. 56.

66. Quoted in Huxley, *Eminem: Crossing the Line*, p. 50.

67. Quoted in Michael Hoyt, "An Eminem Exposé: Where Are the Critics?" *Columbia Journalism Review*, September 2000.

68. Quoted in Hoyt, "An Eminem Exposé."

69. Quoted in Bozza, "Eminem Blows Up."

70. Quoted in Huxley, *Eminem: Crossing the Line*, p. 57.

71. Quoted in Gittins, *Eminem*, p. 26.

72. Quoted in Gittins, *Eminem*, p. 25.

73. Quoted in Huxley, *Eminem: Crossing the Line*, p. 54.

74. Quoted in Huxley, *Eminem: Crossing the Line*, p. 53.

75. Quoted in Gittins, *Eminem*, p. 26.

76. Quoted in Mander, *Access All Areas*, p. 57.

77. Quoted in Mander, *Access All Areas*, p. 60.

78. Quoted in Mander, *Access All Areas*, p. 61.
79. Quoted in Mander, *Access All Areas*, p. 67.
80. Quoted in Mander, *Access All Areas*, p. 66.
81. Quoted in Frank Rich, "The New Elvis? From Cultural Enemy to Mainstream Megastar: Eminem Takes Rap into America's Living Rooms and onto the Big Screen," *New York Times*, December 13, 2002.
82. Quoted in Gittins, *Eminem*, p. 27.

Chapter 4: Professional Success, Personal Failures

83. Quoted in Gittins, *Eminem*, p. 28.
84. Quoted in Weiner, *Eminem: Talking*, p. 84.
85. Quoted in Huxley, *Eminem: Crossing the Line*, p. 65.
86. Quoted in Bozza, "Eminem Blows Up."
87. Quoted in Gittins, *Eminem*, p. 31.
88. Quoted in Gittins, *Eminem*, p. 31.
89. Quoted in Gittins, *Eminem*, p. 32.
90. Quoted in Bozza, "Eminem Blows Up."
91. Quoted in Gittins, *Eminem*, p. 31.
92. Quoted in Gittins, *Eminem*, p. 32.
93. Quoted in Huxley, *Eminem: Crossing the Line*, p. 122.
94. Quoted in Huxley, *Eminem: Crossing the Line*, p. 97.
95. Quoted in Gittins, *Eminem*, p. 32.
96. Quoted in Weiner, *Eminem: Talking*, p. 103.
97. Quoted in Gittins, *Eminem*, p. 35.
98. Quoted in Gittins, *Eminem*, p. 35.
99. Quoted in Huxley, *Eminem: Crossing the Line*, p. 100.
100. Quoted in Gittins, *Eminem*, p. 36.
101. Quoted in Eminem, *Angry Blonde*, p. 4.
102. Quoted in Gittins, *Eminem*, p. 36.
103. Quoted in Gittins, *Eminem*, p. 42.

Chapter 5: Marshall Mathers Takes No Prisoners

104. Quoted in Gittins, *Eminem*, p. 37.
105. Quoted in Weiner, *Eminem: Talking*, p. 66.
106. Quoted in Gittins, *Eminem*, p. 38.
107. Quoted in Weiner, *Eminem: Talking*, p. 68.

108. Quoted in Bozza, "Eminem Blows Up."
109. Quoted in Gittins, *Eminem*, p. 39.
110. Quoted in Gittins, *Eminem*, p. 41.
111. Quoted in Huxley, *Eminem: Crossing the Line*, p. 111.
112. Quoted in Gittins, *Eminem*, p. 41.
113. Quoted in Gittins, *Eminem*, p. 41.
114. Quoted in Huxley, *Eminem: Crossing the Line*, p. 113.
115. Quoted in Huxley, *Eminem: Crossing the Line*, p. 112.
116. Quoted in Gittins, *Eminem*, p. 39.
117. Quoted in Gittins, *Eminem*, p. 39.
118. Quoted in Gittins, *Eminem*, p. 39.
119. Quoted in Gittins, *Eminem*, p. 39.
120. Quoted in Weiner, *Eminem: Talking*, p. 104.
121. Quoted in Eminem, *Angry Blonde*, p. 4.
122. Quoted in Kenyatta, *You Forgot About Dre*, p. 114.
123. Quoted in Gittins, *Eminem*, p. 45.
124. Quoted in Gittins, *Eminem*, p. 45.
125. Quoted in Gittins, *Eminem*, p. 33.
126. Quoted in Gittins, *Eminem*, p. 47.
127. Quoted in Gittins, *Eminem*, p. 47.

Chapter 6: Going Hollywood

128. Quoted in Daniel Fierman, "Acting His Rage," *Entertainment Weekly*, November 8, 2002.
129. Quoted in Richard Schickel, "Eminem's 8 Mile High," *Time*, November 11, 2002.
130. Quoted in Fierman, "Acting His Rage."
131. Quoted in Schickel, "Eminem's 8 Mile High."
132. Quoted in Fierman, "Acting His Rage."
133. Quoted in Fierman, "Acting His Rage."
134. Quoted in Devin Gordon, "Winner by a Mile," *Newsweek*, November 4, 2002.
135. Quoted in Fierman, "Acting His Rage."
136. Quoted in Toure, "*8 Mile* Fact and Fiction," *Rolling Stone*, December 12, 2002.
137. Quoted in Wayne Friedman, "Eminem Picks a New Fan

Base," *Advertising Age*, March 24, 2003.

138. Quoted in Friedman, "Eminem Picks a New Fan Base."

139. Quoted in Mike Clark, "*8 Mile:* Worth the Ride," *USA Today*, November 8, 2002.

140. Quoted in Schickel, "Eminem's 8 Mile High."

141. Quoted in David Ansen, "The Eminem Story," *Newsweek*, November 11, 2002.

142. Kefela Sanneh, "But Seriously: Eminem Tells Slim Shady to Sit Down," *Rolling Stone*, November 28, 2002.

143. *Variety*, December 11, 2002.

144. Quoted in Shaheem Reid, "Eminem: The Gift and the Curse," May 29, 2002. www.mtv.com.

145. Quoted in Reid, "Eminem: The Gift and The Curse."

146. Quoted in Reid, "Eminem: The Gift and The Curse."

147. Kris Ex, "The Eminem Show," *Rolling Stone*, July 4, 2002.

148. David Browne, "The Eminem Show," *Entertainment Weekly*, June 3, 2002.

Chapter 7: Looking Forward

149. Quoted in Rich, "The New Elvis?"

150. Quoted in Rich, "The New Elvis?"

151. Quoted in Rich, "The New Elvis?"

152. Quoted in Edna Gundersen, "'Lose' May Mean Eminem Wins," *USA Today*, March 25, 2003.

153. Quoted in Fierman, "Acting His Rage."

154. Quoted in *People Weekly*, July 8, 2002.

155. Quoted in Diehl, "Will the Real Marshall Mathers Please Stand Up?"

156. Quoted in *People Weekly*.

157. Quoted in *People Weekly*.

158. Quoted in Diehl, "Will the Real Marshall Mathers Please Stand Up?"

159. Quoted in Gittins, *Eminem*, p. 35.

160. Quoted in *People Weekly*.

161. Quoted in *People Weekly*.

162. Quoted in Reid, "Eminem: The Gift and The Curse."

163. Quoted in Rich, "The New Elvis?"

164. Quoted in Diehl, "Will the Real Marshal Mathers Please Stand Up?"
165. Quoted in Rob Sheffield, "People of the Year," *Rolling Stone*, December 12, 2002.
166. Quoted in Sheffield, "People of the Year."
167. Quoted in Michael Fleming, "What Will Follow Film Success for Eminem?" *Daily Variety*, November 15, 2002.
168. Quoted in Fierman, "Acting His Rage."
169. Quoted in Gittins, *Eminem*, p. 5.
170. Quoted in Weiner, *Eminem: Talking*, p. 113.

Important Dates in the Life of Eminem

1970

Debbie Nelson falls in love with and marries Daddy Warbucks bandmate Marshall Mathers Jr. in Kansas City, Missouri.

1972

Debbie Mathers gives birth to Marshall Bruce Mathers III on October 17.

1973

Marshall Mathers Jr. leaves his family to become a hotel manager in California.

1980

Debbie relocates with Marshall to Warren in East Detroit, Michigan.

1983

Marshall is severely beaten by classmate D'Angelo Bailey, resulting in a cerebral hemorrhage; Debbie Mathers decides to move back to Kansas City.

1984

Marshall's uncle Ronnie plays Eminem a song called "Reckless" by Ice T; Marshall decides to become a rapper.

1986

Eminem's half brother, Nathan, is born.

1987

Eminem moves back to Detroit; begins dating Kimberly Scott.

1993

Uncle Ronnie takes his own life; Eminem falls into a deep depression and quits rapping for one year.

1995

December 25: Eminem's daughter, Hailie Jade Mathers, is born.

1996

Infinite is released.

1997

Eminem attends the Rap Olympics in Los Angeles and is discovered by Dr. Dre.

1999

The Slim Shady LP is released on February 23 and goes on to sell 4 million copies. Eminem and Kim are married in June.

2000

May 23: *The Marshall Mathers LP* is released and goes on to sell 8 million copies. On June 3, Eminem is involved in an incident involving Douglas Dail that results in a charge of concealing a deadly weapon. On June 4, Eminem is involved in an incident involving Kim and John Guerra that results in a charge of assault and concealing a deadly weapon. Kim attempts suicide on July 7. In August, she files for divorce.

2001

Eminem's and Kim's divorce becomes final in October.

2002

May 26: *The Eminem Show* is released and goes on to sell 8 million copies. On November 8, the film *8 Mile* is released. It goes on to win great reviews and gross more than $115 million.

For Further Reading

Books

John Bankston, *Eminem (Blue Banner Biography)*. Hockessin, DE: Mitchell Lane, 2003. An informative overview of Eminem's life, aimed at young readers.

Anthony Bozza, *Whatever You Say I Am: The Life and Times of Eminem*. New York: Crown, 2003. A much-anticipated in-depth look at Eminem's life, by the journalist whose career was boosted by his landmark profile of Eminem in 1999.

Scott Gigney, Martin Harper, and Billy Dancer, *His Name Is Eminem*. Surrey, UK: Chrome Dreams, 2001. A well-written overview of Eminem's life, aimed at young adults.

Websites

Eminem World (www.eminemworld.com). This website offers up-to-date headlines about Eminem, archived articles, and an Eminem store.

Official Eminem Website (www.eminem.com). This website offers a biography and up-to-date news listings for Eminem.

Official 50 Cent Website (www.50cent.com). This website offers a biography, up-to-date news, and even a store selling 50 Cent merchandise.

Shady Ltd. (www.shadyltd.com). This official website for Eminem's new clothing line features information on the styles represented, as well as online purchasing.

Works Consulted

Books

Eminem, *Angry Blonde*. New York: Regan Books, 2002. A useful collection of Eminem's lyrics from *The Slim Shady LP, The Marshall Mathers LP*, and *The Eminem Show*, with commentary from the artist.

Ian Gittins, *Eminem*. London: Carlton Books, 2001. A useful all-around biography of Eminem. Unfortunately out of date; cuts off in 2000, prior to *The Eminem Show* and *8 Mile*.

Martin Huxley, *Eminem: Crossing the Line*. New York: St. Martin's Griffin, 2000. Another useful all-around biography of Eminem. Huxley provides a broad array of long, firsthand quotes. Unfortunately out of date, cutting off before *8 Mile*.

Kelly Kenyatta, *You Forgot About Dre: The Unauthorized Biography of Dr. Dre and Eminem*. Phoenix, AZ: BUSTA Books, 2001. This book is divided into three parts: Dr. Dre, Eminem, and their work together. Most of the Eminem information can be found in other sources, but there are some rare quotes and a unique approach.

Hannah Mander, *Access All Areas: Eminem*. London: Michael O'Mara Books, 2001. A minibook of quotes and random facts, aimed at teenage fans. Most quotes are taken from other, more comprehensive sources, but there is a bit of new information.

Chuck Weiner, *Eminem: Talking*. London: Omnibus Press, 2002. Includes an extremely useful and varied compilation of direct quotes from Eminem's interviews.

Periodicals

Charles Aaron, "Chocolate on the Inside," *SPIN*, May 1999.

David Ansen, "The Eminem Story," *Newsweek*, November 11, 2002.

Anthony Bozza, "Eminem Blows Up," *Rolling Stone*, April 29, 1999.

David Browne, "The Eminem Show," *Entertainment Weekly*, June 3, 2002.

Mike Clark, "*8 Mile:* Worth the Ride," *USA Today*, November 8, 2002.

Matt Diehl, "Will the Real Marshall Mathers Please Stand Up?" *CosmoGIRL!*, April 2003.

Kris Ex, "The Eminem Show," *Rolling Stone*, July 4, 2002.

Christopher John Farley, "A Whiter Shade of Pale," *Time*, May 29, 2000.

Suzanne Fields, "Bad Raps: Music Rebels Revel in Their Thug Life," *Insight on the News*, May 21, 2001.

Daniel Fierman, "Acting His Rage," *Entertainment Weekly*, November 8, 2002.

Michael Fleming, "What Will Follow Film Success for Eminem?" *Daily Variety*, November 15, 2002.

Wayne Friedman, "Eminem Picks a New Fan Base," *Advertising Age*, March 24, 2003.

Tom Gliatto, "Sugarless Eminem: With Two Arrests and His Wife Kim's Suicide Attempt, the Controversial Rap Star Faces a Rocky Road," *People Weekly*, July 24, 2000.

Devin Gordon, "Winner by a Mile," *Newsweek*, November 4, 2002.

Edna Gundersen, "'Lose' May Mean Eminem Wins," *USA Today*, March 25, 2003.

Michael Hoyt, "An Eminem Exposé: Where Are the Critics?" *Columbia Journalism Review*, September 2000.

Newsmakers, "Eminem," Issue 2, Gale Group, 2001.

People Weekly, "Eminem: Responsible Citizen," December 30, 2002.

Frank Rich, "The New Elvis? From Cultural Enemy to Mainstream Megastar: Eminem Takes Rap into America's Living Rooms and onto the Big Screen," *New York Times*, December 13, 2002.

Kefela Sanneh, "But Seriously: Eminem Tells Slim Shady to Sit Down," *Rolling Stone*, November 28, 2002.

Richard Schickel, "Eminem's 8 Mile High," *Time*, November 11, 2002.

Rob Sheffield, "People of the Year," *Rolling Stone*, December 12, 2002.

Joel Stein, "Actors: What Does It Take to Morph into a Successful Thespian? Not as Much as You Might Think (Don't Tell Madonna)," *Entertainment Weekly*, December 13, 2002.

David E. Thigpen, "Raps, in Blue: Eminem Rings Up Sales as Well as Controversy," *Time*, April 5, 1999.

Toure, "*8 Mile* Fact and Fiction," *Rolling Stone*, December 12, 2002.

Robin Tyler, "Eminem: Pied Piper of Hate," *Gay & Lesbian Review Worldwide*, May 2001.

Josh Tyrangiel, "The Sound Track of His Life," *Time*, November 11, 2002.

Internet Sources

Associated Press, "Eminem Wins Defamation Lawsuit," October 20, 2003, *Yahoo! News*. www.yahoo.com.

Ted Casablanca, "The Awful Truth," November 14, 2002, *E! Online*. www.eonline.com.

M. L. Elrick, "Eminem's Dirty Secrets," June 25, 2000, *Salon.com*. www.salon.com.

Josh Grossman, "Eminem Makes Like Willy Wonka," September 4, 2003, *E! Online*. www.eonline.com.

Shaheem Reid, "Eminem: Reconstructing Tupac," October 27, 2003. www.mtv.com.

——, "Eminem: The Gift and the Curse," May 29, 2002. www.mtv.com.

Amy Reiter, "A Conversation with Eminem's Mom," February 21, 2001, *Salon.com*. www.salon.com.

Index

Picture Credits

About the Author

Stephanie Lane grew up in Boston and Memphis and currently works as a children's book editor in New York. She lives in Manhattan with her dog, Gabby, and extremely shy cat, Lily.